JUMPING THE TRAIN

An Extraordinary True Story

Charla Avery
Foot Soldier

Dr. Dina V. Avery

Oct 2019

Connie Garn,
Thanks for your
Kindness & support.
Love Always,

For information about special discounts for bulk purchases and to book an event, please contact

A'Nid Global Solutions, LLC

888-367-2643

customersupport@anidglobal.com

Published in the United States by

A'Nid Global Solutions, LLC

Birmingham, AL

Cover Design

Sarco Press

Copyright © 2019 by Dr. Dina V. Avery

ISBN 978-1-08-284124-8

www.dinaavery.com

Contents

To Ben Tanksley, thank you for being the first to see the vision and tap into the spirit of my ancestors. Much love to you and Caroline.

Preface

IT IS HARD TO BELIEVE that I am finally sitting here writing the book I promised my grandfather, Charles D. Avery, Sr. (June 20, 1917 – June 22, 2013). Today is Saturday, June 21, 2014, and it is one of those times when I really miss him. Although I had him in my life for 36 years, you know there is never, ever enough time. Granddaddy died right a year ago and it's time for me to gather all my notes and finish what I promised him. Granddaddy told me a few years before his death that his only regret in life was he did not write a book to chronicle the stories of Ketona, Rushing Spring and our family, the Avery's.

He mentioned to me that he wanted to travel across the globe, telling our oral history, but he let time slip away from him because he was busy working, raising his family and working in our church. He said, "It seems like yesterday that I was just a little boy playing in Rushing Spring, now look at me, I am about to leave here. Time ain't waiting for nobody."

After hearing this, my words to him were, "I think we had better get to work with your story." He laughed and said, "You gonna write my story. Well, we got a lot of work to do. Now listen, I will tell you where to visit and who to talk to. I have already given your Daddy a lot of historical pictures and papers pertaining to us."

You listen to me good, you should add only the people I tell you to put in the book because I know how this thing should go and everybody can't be in the book. I will dig deep and you will dig deep. I give you permission to ask me whatever you want and I will tell you the truth – I promise. Now, are you ready to work, Dr. Avery [chuckling]."

Together, we went to work, I watched and listened to him reflecting back on stories passed down from his paternal grandfather. On this day, I truly had no idea I would start writing this book and my first notes were written on white envelopes with a pencil because these were the only writing tools I could locate at his home. Sometimes while reminiscing, Granddaddy would get tears in eyes, but he rarely would let the tears fall, he would just stop speaking, breathe, turn his head towards his bedroom window and start all over. I could tell that he really missed his family, friends, and neighbors.

He said to me, "I hope this book will remind families and neighborhoods to not let their oral history die – you got to write it down instead of taking memories to the grave. Hell, if you don't write down all of our good stories, they will be gone when I die. It is important for more grandchildren to sit down and listen to old folks."

In his old age, Granddaddy was blind and his legs were very weak. We spent most of our time sitting in his bedroom, just talking or taking long naps. A few times, I sat at the kitchen table with him, sitting at the head of the table with his legs crossed, hands clasped together, and every once in a while he would stroke that long, pointed nose of his. One thing that struck me while he was talking was that his own paternal grandfather told him to not let our family history die and that all Avery's must protect Rushing Spring. Granddaddy said his grandfather said to him, "Boy, you can't let us die. Don't let our stories die."

Granddaddy, specifically told me some stories I must take to my grave. You know those stories that make you speechless, but then again, we all have skeletons in our closet. When telling secrets, he would laugh and say, "Baby, do not write that down because some of these old folks' children may not know – I mean it." I was obedient, but the stories are etched into my memory. Yes, he told me all family secrets, low-down, dirty gossip on the neighbors and church members, the real last names of our neighbors, who dated who, and even told me a few details about himself – Yes, he did. Guess what? He made me promise to keep some things a secret and I will do just that.

It is so funny that even during his final months on earth, we spoke about this book and he said, "Dina, now if you do tell the secrets, don't use their names, OK….." He had a serious look on his face, so hmmmmmmm, I think it is best that I keep the low down dirty secrets, just that---a secret for now.

We spent so much time laughing while talking and I realized he was a walking history book. Really, he started preparing me to write this book when I was a small child sitting in his white, metal patio chair on the front porch. While rocking in the chair, and sitting on his knee, I started learning the family history. I have always been inquisitive, curious and loved history. He taught me to love my last name, but more importantly, he taught me the meaning of my last name, which according to him, Avery's have no fear because we are guided by God. While talking to Granddaddy, I learned that we are still growing up, none of us will ever be perfect, but we can strive to do better.

Granddaddy was spiritual, but not so holy that you did not want to be around him. He knew all of the Books of the Bible and would recite them in chronological and reverse order. He once said to me, "Baby, do you know why Jesus had so many followers? Jesus told you a good story about life, did not take all day to tell you the story, and then went about his Father's business. Some folks go all around the mountain trying to tell one story and it does not take that. If a preacher wants to fill up the church, he needs to follow the lead of Jesus and do not take all day. Rev. Herron would say, "It is a time to speak up, shut up and sit down!"

Although Granddaddy was a God-fearing, spiritual man, he still used a few curse words and even laughed at his own jokes. Whenever he cursed, he would say, "Baby, I am so sorry." He was *always* apologizing and once he got on a roll talking, he could not stop.

Granddaddy was good looking, dark brown, tall, educated, and well-groomed. We, as a family would laugh at him dating. He would tell us that his lady friends liked him because he was nice. I would get so tickled because he never wanted to eat dinner from his lady friends. He would say, "I ain't eating everybody's food." Even, during his last few hours on Earth, he found the strength to talk on the phone to his special lady friend to give his final goodbye.

Even up until he left this world, I was amazed that he was still fluent in French. The week he died, he could still sing the French National Anthem. He never visited France, but knew everything about the French culture. I remember him smiling, saying, "Baby, you got to figure out, how to get the book written in different languages because I want everybody to read it because I bet they are going to love this story."

During one of my visits to his home, he ended our conversation by saying, "Baby, I will not be around when you finish the book, but when you talk about me to people, no crying because you are the one chosen to tell the story. Baby, when you get weak, you gotta suck it up, hold your head up and just do it. I am depending on you."

PART 1
WORDS FROM
CHARLES D. AVERY, SR.

Chapter 1

Early Years

MY NAME IS CHARLES D. AVERY, SR. and I was born on June 20, 1917, to Rector Alexander Avery and Shellie Woods Avery. My father went by the nickname of Alex and he pronounced it as Alec. It is funny now, but almost everyone in the community called him Papa, Paw-Paw or Papa Alec. My mother was known as Mama or Mama Shellie. Nobody called her Grandma, Auntie, none of that, it was simply Mama Shellie.

I was born in our family home located in Rushing Spring, near the church on top of the hill. That is the only house I ever knew us to have while growing up. Our house was built by the men in my family along with a few men from Tarrant City.

When Mama went into labor with me, I was told that all of my family was there at the house and my oldest sister, Senie was in the room with Mama. I remember Mama saying that I was born in the afternoon and I did not have a name for a few days. It was all over Ketona that a baby boy was in Rushing Spring with no name. Can you imagine? A baby with no name, whoever heard of that? Mama always told me that story and she would just laugh about it.

I guess they did not want me to have any ole name. So one day, Papa was walking by the train tracks in Ketona and was stopped by two white men, Charles and David Black. These two men were brothers and they owned the Ketona Lumber Yard located on Ketona Road. While Papa was walking, they said, "Have you named your baby yet?" Papa said he told them, "Nope, we do not know what to name him." So the two brothers said, "You ought to name him after us." Papa liked the sound of the name and that is how I got my name, Charles David.

I grew up with three sisters, Sena, Odell, and Lottie Mae. All of my sisters are now dead. Sena was the oldest girl and we called her Senie and after we got grown with our own kids everybody called her Auntie, even I called her Auntie. All of my sisters had thick, pretty, black hair. I can see Mama now brushing their hair.

I grew up with four brothers, Acie [pronounced A.C.], Verbin, Mathew, and Rector. I was closest to Rector. My brother, Mathew spelled his name with one "t" and we called him Dego. My nickname was Whannie and Rector's nickname was Rec. My younger brother, Verbin's nickname was "Shawt" and no, he was not short. Rec was named after Papa, but Rec on his own decided to change his middle initial to "E" instead of the letter "A" because he said it sounded better. Papa never used Senior after his last name, but I do.

If you put all of us in birth order, let's see, it was Acie, Senie, Rec, Odell, me, then Verbin, Mathew and Lottie Mae. To me, all the boys looked alike. I think the shortest brother may have been Mathew because he was less than six feet tall, but the rest of us were over six feet tall. We got our height from Mama because Papa was short.

We, Avery's have high cheekbones and look at my pointed nose. Papa's side of the family are Black Creek Indians. Look at my skin, it is brown like Papa's skin and in our old age, we, brothers ended up with a baldhead just like Papa. My brother, Mathew stood out because he was very good looking.

When my brothers and I walked into the church over there at Rushing Spring, the old folks would say, "Here come those Avery boys." We would just laugh because we knew we were looking good with our Sunday clothes. Even back then, we wore a clean, white, button-down shirt with a tie, dark suit, black socks, and black shoes. We only had one or two suits, but Mama and Senie took good care of our clothes. Mama always had my sisters looking nice too. We were always clean and we started getting our clothes ready for church on Friday and then on Saturday evening, we got clean for church. You did not wait to the last minute to get ready for church because Sunday was a big day.

MATHEW WAS THE BABY BOY and he stuttered when he talked. I will admit that because of this, we all were too overprotective of Mathew. We did not want anyone to make fun of him. I know you may not believe it, but Mathew did not stutter when he would pray and sing, now how he did that, I do not know. Mathew played the stride piano and was even our church musician over at Rushing Spring Baptist Church.

Mama kept the piano in the front room of the house, so Mathew and Verbin could always practice. Mathew and Verbin both clowned around

17

on the piano and would be moving their body, dancing and rocking—I can see them now. When my brothers played the piano, it was real jazzy and all of us would be rocking, singing and clapping to the beat.

Mathew, Odell, and Verbin loved to cut up dancing. They could swing dance and Papa would join in too. In our house, if you did not play the piano, Mama encouraged us to sing our hearts out because Papa's side of the family loved singing.

Mathew spent most of his time with Verbin and I spent most of my time with Rec. Acie, being the oldest was like a second father to us and he did not let us get into much trouble. Even at a young age, Acie was full of wisdom. We were good children and did not give Mama and Papa many problems. Our parents kept us busy with school, church and working our land. None of us really got whippings because we knew how to behave. We did not have one of those strict households, where you could not have fun. We were blessed because we could sit down and talk to our parents about anything.

AS YOUNG CHILDREN, Senie was in charge of giving all of us a bath. Senie would scrub the hell out of you! She would say, "Mama wants y'all clean, I gotta get you clean." As a small boy, I could not stand for Senie to bathe me. Hell, it was pure torture for all of us. Odell would cut her eyes at Senie during bath time because Odell was tough; you know she did not play. Senie was like a second mother to us because Mama had to work. During the week, yeah we got more than one bath, but again I am telling you, Saturday evening was torture because it seemed like Senie would scrub us even harder because we were getting ready for church.

We did not have our own rooms growing up. The girls slept in the middle room, the boys slept in the back room, and my parents slept in the front room. Senie made sure we went to bed on time.

Our cousins and friends, J.T., Percy "Buddy", Augustus, James "Bubba", and Wesley often spent the night in our back bedroom at least every week or every other week because they lived in Ketona. Our cousin, Felix was always at our house since he lived in Rushing Spring and our cousin, Jesse was often there because he lived on Brown Hill, which is near Rushing Spring. All of them that spent the night were not there at the same time, but it was always at least two or three of them staying on Friday nights and they would go home on Saturday to get ready for church.

WHEN MAMA'S SISTERS and their families came to visit, they would take the front room and the girls' room. My aunts always spent one or two weeks with us during the holidays and summer months. Whenever my aunts came to town, my sisters, brothers, and my parents would pile up in the back room and living room. That was fun for us because we would talk all night and sometimes our cousins would grab a blanket and join us. Back then, we did not have much, but we always enjoyed each other.

Beds back then were not like they are now. I can remember the beds having no headboard and then I can even remember wood & metal headboards in the house. Anybody from my generation will tell you, back then, living in those woods, you had to stay clean because you did not want the bedbugs. Some of the old folks would say, "Don't bring those hanks [bedbugs] into my house."

One time, my Aunt Lozzie got the bedbugs at her house and everybody became scared to enter that house. We continued to visit Aunt Lozzie, but we would check our body and clothes to make sure nothing jumped on us. Back then, if you got bedbugs, they would put kerosene on the box spring to kill them and they would sit the box spring outside for a while away from the house. Sometimes they would just get rid of the box spring.

It was a daily routine for us to work outside and you never knew what you would bring inside the house from the fields. We could not sit on the bed, dirty with our work clothes. Whenever we had been working in the fields, Mama had a special place for us to place our dirty clothes and she did not waste time washing those clothes.

Our house stayed clean at all times. I ain't never lived in a nasty house. Up front in the living room, we had a sofa, about three chairs and there was a small table, a fireplace and a piano with a bench. I think that piano was black. Mama always kept fresh flowers in the house.

We had a dining room with a table and chairs for all of us to eat together in the morning for breakfast and in the afternoon for supper. We only ate twice a day and I still only eat twice a day. Also, in our dining room, there was another table where Mama would keep cakes and different things like nice plates and little knickknacks.

When I was a boy, the kitchen had a black, potbelly, wood-burning stove. You don't know what that is because they don't have those now in the kitchen. We started off using wood in the stove and then started using coal to keep it hot. Let me think, we started off with wood first because I can remember us bringing the wood in the house for the stove.

Papa built a little woodshed outside, where we would keep the coal and wood. We had to pay a man to bring the coal and he would unload it in the woodshed. Even in the 1980s, I think we may have used the same family to bring in the coal. I remember all of us chopping wood and even my Mama could chop wood. Yes, I do remember lighting lanterns in the house and you had to be careful with those lanterns because they had kerosene in them and you did not want the house to go on fire. Near the back door in the kitchen, we had buckets for our water. In the winter months, sometimes the boys slept up front, in the living room because we had to watch the fire inside the fireplace. It was important to watch the fire because you did not want a spark to fly and catch the house on fire. We, brothers, would take turns adding wood to keep the house warm. We had a mantle over the fireplace and even more knickknacks on the mantle. Mama also had a large mirror over the mantle.

Now, the storm shelter is still out there and it is located on the side of the house. That storm shelter ain't going nowhere because it's down in the ground and don't y'all get rid of it. The storm shelter is historical. If I am almost one hundred years old, it has to be older than one hundred. I was told that men in the family built it.

One day, I want you to get somebody to clean the storm shelter and y'all go down in there so you can see it for yourself. When tornadoes would come, we had to get close together and sit on top of each other inside the storm shelter. All of us boys had to keep it clean throughout the year because we did not want snakes to get into it. Rec would even use the top of the storm shelter for his pulpit and act like he was preaching. We crowded around him to play like we were having church.

Sometimes when Mathew would play the piano at home, Rec would have church all over again. Ole Rec would get happy when he preached and all of us would act like we had the Holy Ghost. Mama and Papa watched us and Papa would join in praising God. I'm telling you we had fun at Rushing Spring!

Eating at the dining table with my family was special and there was never a dull moment. We had fun, plenty of fun. We talked, we laughed and Papa, Verbin, Odell, and Rec always cut up at the table by mimicking people. We did not have stern parents. Papa could be silly and tell us funny stories. His favorite story was about jackrabbit and he would make faces like a rabbit while he told it to us.

My brothers, Acie and Rec could cook like my Mama. They spent a lot of time in the kitchen with her. I have always loved sweet potatoes, so Rec always baked me a sweet potato pie and I did not have to share it. It was my pie, all to myself. We always grew sweet potatoes in our garden.

Mama and Papa loved all of us, but Acie was extra special to them probably because he was their first-born. Acie was special to us too because he carried himself like he had a million dollars in his pocket. Acie knew he was somebody and ended up marrying a school teacher!

MY FAVORITE TIME with Papa, Grandpaw, and my brothers was hunting on our land. We would go into those woods at Rushing Spring and have good time hunting. From the time we were little boys, we received a pocket knife and we even received our own shotguns as we grew older. We never horse played with our guns. Our guns were for hunting only. Odell would sometimes go with us to hunt. When hunting, you got to be quiet and watch your surroundings.

I can remember we kept noticing our vegetables missing from the garden and we knew it had to be an animal coming off that hill. Well, we were little boys and we joined Papa and Grandpaw to go hunting. We went deep in the woods to hunt squirrels and rabbits. A coyote came up near where Mathew was standing and that coyote circled Mathew. Grandpaw told us not to move, but Verbin pulled out his pocket knife. Verbin was a little boy and you know, he was not scared of that coyote, and threw his knife, but missed the coyote.

The coyote became agitated and ran away. That was the first time and only time, Papa yelled at any of us. He had to get onto Verbin because we were told not to move, but that was Verbin's way of protecting my brother. Papa made all of us continue to hunt that day; I guess he did not want us to get a fear of hunting. Mama would cook whatever we killed.

Another thing, we did was pick blackberries for Mama. We loved to grab our bucket and climb those trees picking berries – it was fun. Mama was good at baking blackberry pies.

RUSHING SPRING has always been a nice place. There were houses all around in Rushing Spring. The houses were little shacks and almost everybody there was family and if they were not family, we called them family. Rushing Spring is part of the Ketona community. Tennessee Coal, Iron and Railroad Company (TCI) brought in workers and provided them housing in the Ketona neighborhood.

Next to Rushing Spring, is a neighborhood called Brown Hill and it is not far from a rock quarry. Family on Papa's side owned Brown Hill and Mama's sister, Nelly married into the Brown family. We spent a lot of time up there with Aunt Mamie Peterson, Aunt Carrie Brown, and Aunt Nelly

Brown. Everybody on Brown Hill was either a Brown or a Peterson and they are all related to us Avery's. I can remember walking with my brothers to Brown Hill to get our chickens. Brown Hill had chickens everywhere! They also sold mules. Brown Hill made good money off their animals and vegetables. Brown Hill ain't never been broke! Everybody on Brown Hill could work all day and night.

Now down at Rushing Spring, we worked, but not like them. Everybody from Brown Hill went to Rushing Spring Baptist Church. We always spent time with our cousins from Brown Hill; I was closest to Jesse Peterson.

All around Rushing Spring are springs and that's why it is called Rushing Spring. When I was able, I tried to keep the springs clean and when I got old, I paid for somebody to clean it because that is what I am supposed to do because of love for my parents and Grandpaw.

I remember water flowing in the spring from the hill and it was pretty to see. Now, if you go up to the old church, to the wooded area by the parking lot, there is a spring where we helped Mama wash clothes. Sometimes, she would have to get the spring water hot by boiling it in a large pot so she could wash clothes. My siblings and I even played in that spring water. You see that spring water is good and real cold. I grew up on that water!

Papa was like a handyman, he wasn't doing too much, but he built outhouses and was good with his hands. Almost everybody had an outhouse or a slop jar because that was where you had to use the bathroom so Papa was popular. Mama washed clothes and ironed clothes for a living. She washed clothes for many white families from Ketona, Tarrant,

Eastlake, and Woodlawn. All of us would help her with laundry. Wait, I do remember Papa taking just a few jobs as a laborer and had to go downtown to work.

There was one customer Mama had that was a white woman and she was crazy about me. She would even sneak and give me her husband's clothes when I was a teenager. I needed nice clothes since I attended Catholic School. You see, I would have to help deliver and pick up the clothes for Mama. This white lady was a school teacher and she knew I was smart. That nice white lady was killed in a car accident. When Mama told me that woman died, I could not stop crying, I cried for days. She was the nicest white lady, I ever met and she would help me with my homework because I was trying to better myself. It hurts right now to talk about her.

Now, over by Ketona nursing home there was a customer, who was as mean as a rattlesnake! I went over there to drop off clothes that Mama had washed and ironed, and she said, "I am going to pay you to do some yard work." I worked all day, I mean all day, and she did not want to pay me. So, I grabbed as many vegetables and apples as I could and placed them in the clothes basket. I was wrong, but I considered that my pay [chuckling].

WHEN CHRISTMAS CAME, all of Mama's sisters would be at our house. No, we did not get toys at Christmas. We received cakes, pies, and one wagon. All of us played with that one wagon all day. When working in the fields, the wagon came in handy. We took turns to pull the wagon up and down our hill.

As we got older, Odell's kids, Sue and Snook lived with us. It was important for all of us to give them several gifts from Santa Claus. All of us would sit on the floor and play with them on Christmas Day. When Snook received his first toy shotgun, we watched Papa teaching him how to aim and shoot.

Growing up, we all loved riding and taking care of our horses. Our favorite horse was named Dan. We had Dan for a long time. My sister Odell could ride a horse just like us. She was not afraid of anything. We picked up our love for horses from Grandpaw. As I am talking, I still remember when Grandpaw bought the buggy for the horses. We went with him over to Eastlake to the area where today, they sell cars. Over in that area, they sold buggies for your horses. Grandpaw saw the buggy he wanted and went up to the white salesman and said, "I want this buggy." The salesman said, "How are you going to buy this buggy?" Grandpaw pulled out his cash and just looked at him. The salesman took the money and we left Eastlake with that buggy for our horses. All of us could fit in it too. When we got the buggy back to Rushing Spring, everybody came out to look at it. The buggy meant everybody in Rushing Spring and Ketona had something to ride in.

I had a good childhood and I have no complaints. I thank God for growing up in Rushing Spring because I was with my family. Really, being black, we were well-off because we had land, a house, horses, mules, cows, pigs, goats, chickens, and we grew our own vegetables. The most important thing was the church was right by our house. What else did we need?

Mama had steady money from washing and Papa had money here and there from odd jobs, but my Grandpaw had steady money because he sold vegetables and was a janitor down at the courthouse. Sometimes, he trained horses for the whites. Grandpaw even rented rooms to people. Back then, I will say that everybody pulled their money together and that is why it seemed like we had more than enough.

Then, think about this, how many blacks went to Catholic school – I did. Back then, a lot of people my age went to at least the sixth or eighth grade, but Mama and Papa sacrificed. Rec wanted to preach and I was smart so we went to Catholic School for a while. It was not easy, giving us money to get downtown to attend school. I decided to leave St. Mark Catholic School because I wanted to finish at Hooper City High School. Roy Brewster was one of my closest friends, who later became my brother-in-law, and he also attended St. Mark with me before going to Hooper City High School.

After graduating from high school, I went to Miles College where I played basketball and football. I wanted to become a school teacher. I can remember Papa coming to see me play and I broke my arm during the football game. I wanted to show Papa that I was a good football player. Soon after that, I stopped playing football.

I had to leave Miles College because Mama asked all the boys to go to work because of World War II. Acie and I told her we would go to the coal mine to work. You know how Verbin liked to joke, he said, "Mama, Verbin Avery ain't working in no mine for nobody – it is dark in there" and he kept walking right out the back door. We all laughed because that was our Verbin.

At that time, Rec did not go with me and Acie to the coal mine. Acie worked down deep in the mine and I was in the top house, I never went down inside the coal mine. I did not last long working there, but at least I tried.

After I left the coal mine, Acie continued to work there and the money really helped our household. My sisters and brothers continued to help sell vegetables and wash clothes. During that time, everybody in Rushing Spring and Ketona worked together and we did not miss a beat during World War II. Today, you would say we were hustling, just trying to make it.

I will say this, we ain't never begged anyone for money. We all worked hard. The Bible says, "If a man will not work, he shall not eat!" Believe me, that is a true statement. Baby, you got to work hard and not expect anyone to give you a hand out because you are having hard times – everybody got their own bills. When you pray, ask God to keep you in your right mind with good health so you can work.

WRITE DOWN THIS FUNNY STORY. One day, Mama and Papa left us home alone and Odell wanted to wrestle Rec. Odell whipped Rec's butt and almost pulled his ear off. Rec's ear started to bleed and we panicked. None of us knew what to do and I know this sounds crazy, but his ear was almost hanging so we slapped some black coal on it so Mama and Papa wouldn't see the blood. When they came home, we acted as if nothing happened and my parents never found out about that.

Another memory is back then, there was a prison in Ketona and the prisoners would escape all the time. One Saturday, all of us children were sitting in the front room and the door was always unlocked, and do you know a prisoner ran into our house through the front door while we were sitting in the living room near the front door. The prisoner ran from the front door and out the back door. The police were running right behind the prisoner. All of our eyes looked at the front door and our eyes followed them out the back door with our mouths wide open, we did not move – it is funny now, but it was not then.

DOUBLE CHECK ME, I think Mama had about a third grade education and Papa stopped attending school around the second grade. Although my parents did not have much education, they pushed us toward education. My parents sacrificed for us to have a better life. Verbin received his degree from Alabama State University and I attended Miles College. Senie did not get a degree, but she received her certification or some type of training to teach people how to read and write. She spent time teaching in Montgomery, AL. She only did it for a little while and came back home with us. When Senie got back home from teaching, she would continue to help Mama wash clothes. I went to see Verbin coach a few games while he was at Alabama State and I went to the house where he lived in Montgomery, AL.

AS A TEENAGER, MATHEW WAS DRAFTED in World War II and served as a Seaman for the U.S. Coast Guard. My brother Mathew is still lost at sea. Check with Charles Jr, but I think Mathew was over in New Guinea when the incident happened.

My first cousin, Felix Avery and a man whose last name was Brown from Tarrant City were on the ship with Mathew and told us everything that happened the day he went missing. In life, you learn how to deal with death because life goes on, but dealing with Mathew's death was hard and it is still hard to deal with. Mathew's name is on a memorial wall over in the Philippines.

Mama received money from Mathew's death and when some of the whites in Tarrant City found out about it, they took money from Mama. The whites told her that if she complained about it, they would kill her sons. Mama never spoke about it to Papa or any of us until years before she died.

When my parents were alive, there was a prayer service for Mathew at the church, but we never had a memorial service. As an old man, I may have been in my seventies or eighties; I told Rec and Verbin that we needed to have a memorial for Mathew before we all die. They both agreed. I contacted Verbin first because he and Mathew would call themselves twins, but they were not. Next, I called Rec and we set the date. My sisters were in no shape to attend the graveside service because of their health and we brothers only wanted it to be the siblings present, but Charles Jr. was there because he helped get everything set-up at the cemetery.

We got together on a Saturday morning and had a graveside service for Mathew. This marked our final goodbye to our brother. We did not say much, but I could hear my heartbeat and I can hear it now while talking about this. Together, we prayed and had a tombstone for Mathew placed near Mama and Papa's gravesite at Shadowlawn.

I do not ever want the family to forget Mathew. I want them to remember that although he stuttered, he did not let that stop him. He was determined! Mathew could sing, pray, play the piano, got his schoolwork and served his country. Mathew always greeted everyone with a smile and he was a helper. Mathew was just humble and it ain't nothing bad I can say about him — that's the truth!

I gave Mathew's medals to Charles Jr. and when Charles Jr. is no longer here, y'all take care of those medals because Mathew had no children. I have a picture somewhere in this house of Mathew. Senie always kept a picture of Mathew on top of the piano because that was his favorite spot in the house.

Chapter 2

Growing Older with Wisdom

WHEN I THINK OF GROWING OLDER, it is a blessing, but it is pure hell on your body. I like to run and I cannot run like I did as a young man. I still believe in staying healthy. That is why, I don't eat all day, but I do have a sweet tooth. When I am here in bed, I exercise my legs and I can still lift my legs pretty high. I exercise my arms and move my body from side-to-side. When you are independent for so long, getting older is something else, but I'm thankful because my children still make sure I have my manhood. I am still living in my own home, y'all check on me all day and Charles Jr. keeps me updated on my money.

Really, I keep breathing for my children and grandchildren. I worked hard to see all of you make it. When a man can say all of his children and grandchildren stepped foot on a college campus –that's a blessing! My parents and grandparents pushed all of us to get some type of education and then I helped my children push their children. No one can take your education from you. It is better to be overqualified than underqualified. If you do not get a degree, at least get a certificate or trade. You must have a skill that you enjoy. Remember, if you do not get the job you want, do not let it be because of your education. If they do not want to hire you, move on to the next job and go get what God wants you to have.

WHEN ALL OF YOU WERE GROWING UP, your grandmother did most of the discipline because I had to work. Even when I retired, I did odd jobs for extra change and that was because of y'all. Granddaddy has never been a lazy man! My children and grandchildren will never say, I did not provide for them.

It may have been selfish of me, but I prayed that none of my children would end up on welfare. I wanted all of you to have more than enough. Remember, God will provide if you just trust Him. I always look to the hill from whence cometh my help – all of my help comes from God.

In life, times might get hard, but you keep going. An Avery can handle just about anything. Why? We know God and we just don't know Him, we trust Him. In life, when you get out of one thing, here comes another and another, but hell you just keep moving. You hear me? Keep praying and God got you.

It was not easy working on my job, but did I stop going to work? No! Did I throw a fit and get mad on my job? No! I knew that I was working to provide for my family. I took a whole lot on my job, but today, don't you take it.

Let's go back to why you need an education. With your education and all these computers and thangs, you can create your own job. What are you scared of? If George Washington Carver took a sweet potato and changed the world, what the hell are people afraid of – I do not understand. If you can, one day be your own boss, but be an honest boss.

Listen to me good. In life, you will find out that some people cannot handle power and authority. The key to success is being humble. When a person gets greedy and not humble, they will tumble. You should never let money rule you, you should rule the money. Be careful, who you tell your next moves to because everybody does not want you to go higher and even people you are close to are waiting on you to fail. Even when preparing for this book, we got to hush because someone will want to take over.

Remember now, when you are the boss, be kind to the people that work for you. I am telling you again, you never know, who will have to help you in this life. Some people think, since they are the boss, they can talk to you any type of way, but it does not work like that. When it is time to set rules, do not move too fast and let God lead you. Sometimes, we have bumps in the road, but consider that a life lesson. God has a way of preparing us for what is ahead in our life.

WHEN I COULD NO LONGER SEE with my eyes, did I give up? No! Losing my eyesight really does not bother me because every once in a while, God will allow me to see or catch a shadow of something. Then, all of you serve as my eyes, so I don't worry about my eyesight.

Now, if I could see, I would be traveling to see my great-grandchildren. I think I have up to seven great-grandchildren. I have Kelsey, Ashleigh, Bri-Bri, Kay-Kay, Jayla, Avery & Seth - six girls and one boy! If I could see and had my strength, I am telling you, I would be back and forth from Georgia, Michigan, and Texas, with my great-grandchildren. You would hardly see me here in Alabama. My grandchildren got to travel with me, but I do wish I could actually see my great-grandchildren in their different school activities.

You know my Seth is something else. That is my boy! When Seth comes here, he loves to see that trains pass by my bedroom window. When he was here, he saw the train outside and I pretended I could see it too. He said, "Granddaddy, the train is here! You see it!" I said, "Yes, Baby! Granddaddy can see the train! Look at it go!" I do not think he knows I cannot see. I love that boy, but I love all mine.

My heart is happy to know that soon, Kelsey and Ashleigh will soon graduate from college. My girls are doing it, they are really doing it. It makes me feel good to know they are going to have a college degree, but all mine will make it because the seed has been planted.

Watch this, your grandmother and I raised our children with the help of grandparents, then we helped our kids with their kids, now I am on my third generation and I get to sit back because the seed is already in all of you. I am thankful none of mine keep me up at night worried because they are out there doing something wrong. That ain't the way to live; no one wants that stress. Stress will kill you and God will tell you when to distance yourself from the one causing you stress.

I AM ALWAYS HERE LISTENING to the news. I know everything that is going on in the world. I must pray for people everywhere. Yes, I still get on my knees to pray. When I pray, I start off by thanking God, then I make my requests known to God, next I pray for my children, my grandchildren, my great-grandchildren, my future generations, all my nieces and nephews, the church, the children of Ketona & Rushing Spring, mankind and on and on. Yes, I pray for a long time.

I don't need anyone to help me to get on and off my knees to pray because you see, God does that. Even when I am in bed, I pray. When I eat – I pray. When I am walking – I pray. When I raise my right hand to grab my water – I pray. You gotta pray all day.

Growing up, I listened to Papa and Grandpaw pray. I remember when Grandpaw would be in the fields working and he would sing and pray all day. Baby, you got to stay prayed up. When you stay prayed up, God will never let anything sneak up on you. When something ain't right with y'all or the church, I already know about it because God allows me to see it. I see every detail. When I die, I want all my children and grandchildren to remember that I love you and I pray for all of you. All of you have made me proud! I cannot tell you how proud I am.

Now, have I been a perfect man? No. Have I messed up? Yes. Do I still mess up at my age? Yes. You all see me as being perfect, but Daddy ain't perfect and no one is perfect, only Jesus was perfect. Remember you must have sense enough to know when to repent and pray. That's what you got to do, repent, pray and do better. When you pray, don't keep worrying God about the same thing. You pray, let it go and keep moving. Why? Because we have Faith! If you have faith, you can always do the impossible.

I ALWAYS TAUGHT y'all to read. You will not know anything if you do not read. I have always kept books in this house and books are not for decoration. Reading will allow you to give yourself a vision and then you can say, "I can do that too."

Anyone, who wants to grow wise should pull out their Bible and read the Book of Proverbs. Proverbs will provide you with wisdom and teach you some common sense. When you read the Bible, you first got to have the right attitude. Some people will pick up the Bible and try to find fault. People, who want to find fault love to say, "Those church folks", but church folks got to be a good example too. It is okay to have a discussion over the Bible, but never argue over the Bible. Before you read the Bible, it is important to pray for wisdom and understanding.

AS YOU GROW OLDER, you do not want anyone to ever label you as a fool. Fool is one of the most horrible words for you to call anyone, but I am going to tell you what defines a fool. A fool does not follow the directions of God. A fool is a person that you cannot tell them anything. A fool does not want to listen to instruction from anyone. A fool has all the answers to everything and will not listen to reason. Listen to this, a fool can sometimes not care because they think their way is perfect, even when it ain't. Only ungodly people do not care if they act like this.

Remember, never argue with those, who think they know everything because a lot of times they act ugly, in order for you to join in to cut up right along with them. Do not give them what they want and do not mess up your name! I will tell you another thing, anybody that cuts up, fussing at our church or any church has a serious problem and they define the meaning of what is considered a fool because they are not obeying the teachings of God. The dirt you throw out, in this life, you will get it thrown right back at you. What goes around will surely come back around. We must try to do better.

Watch how you live your life. All of you need to watch how you treat people and especially the church. When you get time, read James 1: 19 because it tells you about how you must be quick to listen, slow to speak, and slow to become angry. Read it for yourself – it's there!

I have witnessed a lot of times when men are becoming men, they do not listen. They will make careless mistakes simply because they do not want to listen to those with wisdom. Sometimes growing up, you can have too much pride, but that ain't the way to live.

I will never be labeled by anyone as someone, who does not listen because even today, I want to surround myself with Godly wisdom. We must remember to never be quick-tempered. Being ready to raise hell and fighting ain't never solved a problem. A real man knows how to talk peacefully and remain even-tempered.

Even with my shotguns, I know right now, who to pass them down to, based on your temper. If you are quick-tempered, you will end up in jail, hungry, no money or dead. You will find that those with a bad temper will rarely say, "I am sorry, please forgive me." Never, ever, go to bed mad at anyone and read the Bible on forgiveness.

In this life, we need each other, whether you like it or not. You cannot live in this world and try to live like you do not need anyone. Some people have a chip on their shoulders because they are unhappy about little things and then you do not even understand, why they are so upset. When you start cutting off family and those you love, first look at yourself and make sure you are doing what is right. If you are not led by God when making decisions like that, it will come back to bite you. I am telling you, God sees everything we do! Pray to God to be wise, full of love and have a heart of forgiveness.

I want this in the book..........when you become old in age like me, please stop being mean and low down to people! Some old folks do not care how they speak to people, you must be careful with your words. Old folks forget that they too can end up going to hell.

Old folks must realize when it is time to sit down or step aside, in order for the next generation to lead. We see this often in the church and on jobs. Even when we sit down, we still can provide wisdom and guidance, but we cannot take over everything. Old people, like me need to remember, we do not know everything, so we should stop acting like it! Old people must listen and accept some new ideas from young people. I have been at Rushing Spring for over nine decades and change has occurred in each decade.

Old folks must be nice and say "thank you" because people do not have to be nice to you. Watch this though, my sons and daughters-in-law help take care of me because I know how to act. Nobody is rushing to move me in the nursing home because I am mean. All of my girls live out-of-town, but God blessed me with my daughters-in-law, Mary and Jerri and they enjoy seeing about me.

Think about what I am saying, baby, I don't have to cook, clean up the house and my sons keep me clean. Why? Because I am nice and when I am wrong, I am man enough to say, "I am sorry." Now just because I am nice does not mean I will not speak up for myself when it is time, but even when you do speak up, you should still be even-tempered. And to all old folks, if your children tell you to take a bath, please take a bath! When you are old like me, you cannot smell like you once did. Hell, old folks gotta listen to their children!

EVEN AS AN OLDER DEACON over at the church, I had to learn when to sit my butt down! My heart is in the church and I was born by the church, so the way I feel about different situations that happen will be different from someone just walking in there.

I remember going to a Deacon Meeting on a Saturday morning and I was sitting next to J.T. Together, we got so angry at someone and I said to myself, this is my last Deacon Meeting. I was around seventy-two years old when that happened. I stopped going to those meetings because on that day, I felt myself almost have a heart attack. My head and my chest starting hurting all because of a man's words about the church and the future of the church. He was being very harsh and I did not want to retaliate inside the church.

I had to use my wisdom to know when to sit down and keep my mouth shut because at that moment if I had opened my mouth, it would have been ugly. All of the Deacons that grew up with me came down to my house and I told them, "I am done with meetings because I ain't acting ugly." All of us had to calm down because we were so angry. You cannot be around people or events that make you angry because you may end up doing something that you have no business. It can take one minute to get yourself in trouble and sometimes a lifetime to get out of trouble – it ain't worth it.

This is the lesson I want you to learn from that example. Wisdom spoke to me and said my health at seventy-two years old was more important than getting upset at a meeting. A wise man knows when to speak, when to keep the peace, and when to sit down. Now my sons are on the Deacon Board and yeah, that makes me feel good because they are going to think like Daddy. And when you think like Daddy, you are thinking like my Daddy and his Daddy. You get where I am going.

WHEN I RAISED MY CHILDREN, there were times when I as Daddy had to put my foot down. When you raise children, first you must be a good example. You must show your children, how to pray, how to work hard, and how to take care of their family. Now my kids ain't perfect, but I did my part in raising them. Now, what I taught my children goes back to what I learned over at Rushing Spring. One thing, I stressed to my children and grandchildren, do not get on that hay [drugs]. I do not want y'all strung out because it will mess up your entire life.

Like I said before, if a man will not work, he shall not eat—remember that. Now I'm going to take it further......a man that thinks he knows everything will self-destruct and then his children will sometimes act up just like him. The worse whipping you can get is one from God. God knows how to grab your attention when you do not listen. I have seen it happen too many times.

Not long ago, we once had a preacher to come to the church to preach for Father's Day. Our Pastor did not preach that Sunday. In the sermon, he spoke on how men treat their children by being tough and mothers show more love. As I listened, I sat there and said, "Lord thank you for Rushing Spring." I do not know anything about being a mean father and I grew up seeing men show love to their family.

As the man preached, I felt sorry for him because I hope he does not pass that behavior to his children. That hill over there taught me about love. Every time, I see my children and grandchildren, I say, "I love you" and we hug. Ain't that right? My grandparents did the same thing to us. Be thankful that in this family, we show each other love. My wife did not let anyone enter this house without giving them a hug. Everybody needs love and kindness and if they say they do not, they are lying and they are full of themselves.

Although I am an old man, there is never a day I don't think of my parents. Lord, I miss them. I miss all of them that have gone on. Lord knows that I miss visiting my parents. I can remember when I got off work, I would run from Ketona to Rushing Spring and my children would be behind me. That's love! All of you still stay under me right now all of the time because of love. Don't you know I feel good when my grandchildren drive in or fly in to see me – it is all because of love! Read your Bible, love will change anything. When a family disagrees, love can smooth things out.

I want you to know I was married to Eula for forty-eight years. Yeah, I still miss her. I miss talking with her and traveling. I still love her, but we were blessed to stay together that long. Another thing, I showed my wife love.

I pray all of you end up marrying the one God wants you to have. Another thing, do not let any preacher tell you that it is wrong to divorce because that is a lie. Yes, when you marry, you want it to work and you try, but I do not go along with fighting and calling folks out their names. Sometimes a divorce can be a blessing and then the next go-round, you may end up with your soulmate. When a man cannot love his wife, like Christ loved the Church, it will never work.

Remember, God knows what He is doing. Don't ever rush into marriage; it will happen in God's perfect time. If a preacher tells you or any woman to stay there in a bad marriage and she is getting knocked in the head, you tell the preacher to go live in that marriage and get knocked in the head. Better yet, get your purse, leave and do not even listen to him.

AND YOU KNOW WHAT PREACHERS like to talk about? Tithing, tithing, tithing, that ten percent. Y'all know my view on tithing. If I just stuck to giving ten percent that would not be as much as what I currently give to the church over there. If a preacher would focus on teaching the members to get their heart right and how to live for God, the church would overflow with people and money.

Baby, remember giving is a process. Life will teach you how to give – trust me. Because when you start living right according to the Word and as you grow spiritually, then you want to start giving God your all. Then, you will want to be a cheerful giver by giving more than ten percent and you will want to give God your service by working in the church and outside the church. I give way over ten percent and a lot of us old folks give over ten percent because our heart is in serving God. I do not like hearing about ten percent because some preachers ain't teaching it right, but that is just Granddaddy's opinion. When teaching tithing, preachers got to go deeper than just telling you to give ten percent.

When I really started saving, this is what I did. In my checking account, I always keep $1,000.00 ready for each child because no matter how old your child is they might need something. So for me, that is $1,000.00 multiplied by five kids. I always keep $500 cash in this house that I can get to because something may happen in the middle of the night. Then, whatever you payout in bills each month, you need to multiply it by twelve months and put that amount in savings and do not touch that amount for nobody – I do not care, who it is.

Over time, the goal should be to have at least one year's salary in the bank, but it takes time. Remember don't touch your savings for you to live because you cannot depend on these jobs. If you lose a job, you will not be all upset when you have money in the bank. You can live off your savings while you look for another job. Also, men need at least $100.00 cash in their pocket at all times.

Remember to watch family folks because you always will have that one person with their hand out all the time. Watch them because they will use you if you let them. If you let them use you, then that is your fault. If a person begs all the time, that ain't your problem, but let the Spirit lead you, but do not get used because they can go to work or get a second job. You got to be careful, especially when you are single and making a little money. Different ones in the family will think they can come and borrow, borrow, borrow, but do not start it – I mean it, do not start it! You are not responsible. The Lord will tell you when it is time to give to someone.

Always keep your business straight. Get you a good lawyer to take care of your business. Another thing, you got to keep your business updated because people will change on you. My business stays updated; you can ask your daddy. Now with me, I ain't waiting until I am dead for my children to get little something. I want my children to enjoy while I am here.

When you die, leave the church little something. Okay, you and Tommy do not have kids, but you have Kelsey, Ashleigh, Jayla, Kay-Kay and the church. Then, you do not know, who God will send to care for you. Time will tell you, who should be over your business. Even though, I am blind and stay in this house, Charles Jr. tells me about every dime I have. I call him "Boss Man" because he looks out for my business. You know what is funny, he makes sure my wallet has cash money and I do not even leave the house.

I EXPECT YOU AND TOMMY to continue working in the church. You owe it to your ancestors. They worked hard for that church. Now, my other grandchildren are too far away, but if they come back here, and even if they join somewhere else, they better make time to work at Rushing Spring. I expect all of my nieces and nephews too to work at our church. Even if you all hear that Ebenezer Baptist Church up the street needs help, I expect everyone to give money because they are family.

I pray that the families over at Rushing Spring can stay together, but one thing for sure, I want an Avery there somewhere. If the church ever has a fallout, just know all those angels are looking over the church. The church will be okay. Yeah, members may fallout, but the Rushing Spring will roll-on. God's house will always be okay.

IF FORMER SLAVES HAD THE VISION to form Rushing Spring and had very little, don't you know God got us? When I was growing up, I was taught that my great-grandparents [Rev. Alexander and Hannah Goins] would let those, who were once slaves live on that land. Sometimes you hear us call Rushing Spring, *Holy Ground*, and yeah it is. And when something is Holy, you may shake it, but everything will be alright because you ain't gonna break it. They have called that place *Holy Ground* since I was a boy.

As a boy, there was a woman dressed in all white that would come to pray at the spring near the old church. We did not know, who she was and she did not want to talk to us. She did not even accept food when we offered it to her. All she wanted to do was pray and drink the spring water. We would watch her and wonder, "Where did this lady come from?" Praying on that hill ain't just started, that is why I do not want anyone to worry about Rushing Spring because prayer has sustained us this long and will continue.

You asked me the meaning of life is short. Well, life is short. It seems like yesterday that I was a boy and now I am an old man. I have buried all my siblings, most of my friends and I am the last man standing from my era in Ketona. I sit back and think about all the good times. I rarely cry, but oh what a good ride it's been for me – God knows I am thankful!

I am thankful that so far I have not had to bury my children and grandchildren. The hardest death I ever endured was my brother, Rec. I think Rec died in 2003. I usually can handle things like a man, but not on that day. I can honestly say that when Rec died, a part of me died with him. Remember, when Rec died, all of my children were home and I had to be taken to the hospital. It was like the wind was knocked out of me. Rec's daughter, Gwen even came to see about me. I could not handle Rec's death, but wisdom whispered to my soul and said, "Do not even try to attend the funeral." When Rec's body arrived at Rushing Spring, I viewed the body and came right back home. I knew and accepted my limitations.

When Verbin died about three years later, I wept like a baby because I became the last surviving sibling and I had no more brothers and sisters here with me. Verbin and I spent a lot of time talking and even though both of us were old men, he depended on my advice. When Verbin entered my house, he would be loud and say, "Hey Charles Avery, Verbin Avery is here!"

My wife's cousin, Aunt Bessie lives up in the front part of this house. One day, she overslept. I could tell what time it was because of the television shows. I waited and jokingly, I said, "Hell, I hope Bessie ain't dead in this house." Do you know how many people have died in this house? I got my cane and slowly walked up front and started calling her name and she did not move. I knocked on the door and Bessie still did not move. When I tapped her on the shoulder, she jumped and I said, "Hell Bessie, I thought you died on me!" You know I am a jokester and we both laughed.

MY RIDE HAS BEEN GOOD. I just want you all to be okay because I must die. You can tell everybody your Granddaddy is not afraid to die. Tom and Charles Jr. will cry more than my girls when I am gone, but they will be okay with time because they will be busy working in the church. My Dot will be the one that has to keep the family together. I still want family gatherings to continue.

The only person I am concerned about when I die is Doris Jean. You know I nicknamed her my *Sapphire*. I know all of you love me, but I want y'all to talk on the phone with Doris Jean when I am gone because she calls me all day. Doris Jean starts calling early in the morning and y'all better answer her call when I am gone. Carolyn & Gerald will be okay as long as they can sleep and drink coffee [laughing]. Tell Gerald, I truly thank him for looking out for my three girls and I want him to continue.

Chapter 3

Grandpaw

YOU KNOW, ALL OF Y'ALL ON THESE COMPUTERS looking up my folks, but all you have to do is call me and I will be glad to tell you. I love history and that computer ain't gonna tell you the nicknames, the secrets, and stuff I witnessed and heard for myself with my own eyes. Just like y'all looking up stuff, I asked questions directly to some of the folks, you are looking up.

Let me tell you about Grandpaw. We did not say Grandpa. You gotta put emphasis on Paw and drag it out like this Grandpaaaaw. Grandpaw's sons called him Paw. Grandpaw's parents named him Alexander Avery because his Daddy was named Alexander Avery. Do not get Alexander Avery confused with Alexander Goins. The name Alexander is a family name on Grandpaw's side and Grandmaw's side.

My Grandpaw did not keep the name Alexander Avery because when he left the Bibb County plantation, he changed it to James Manual Avery and most folks around here called him Manual. Grandpaw's brother was Uncle Lee. Uncle Lee's real name was Wesley Avery. They both were born in Alabama down at the Avery Plantation in Bibb County, AL.

Grandpaw's mother was Sylvia Avery. Grandpaw and Uncle Lee did not pronounce her name as Sylvia, they would say, "Sevie". You gotta remember the way they pronounced words back then is different from today. Sylvia Avery went by the nickname of Retta. Grandpaw and Uncle Lee called their mama, Ma Retta.

Ma Retta's mama was Lide. They both called their grandmother, Ma Lide. Today, we say "Lydia". I cannot remember them talking about Ma Lide's husband; I do not know too much about him.

Now although Ma Retta and Ma Lide were dead when I was a boy, you would not know it because Grandpaw and Uncle Lee talked about them all the time like they were still living. I do remember them saying Ma Lide's parents were Sampson & Mamie Avery from Chesterfield County over in South Carolina. I was taught that Ma Lide told Ma Retta that our family was split up in Chesterfield County when the slave master moved to Bibb County, Alabama. Ma Lide was still able to relocate to Bibb County with her parents.

Now this is important, the Avery slave master lived in North Carolina first before living in South Carolina and from South Carolina, he moved to Bibb County. Grandpaw often said, "We gotta go to Chesterfield one day and find our folks." He told me stories about Ma Lide's parents living in Chesterfield County with the Avery slave master. Grandpaw never made it there, but I should have gone there when I was driving, but y'all go one day. I bet you can find them. I just know some of our folks are still there in Chesterfield. When you do your research, remember if you lived on the plantation together, I learned that you called each other family, even if you were not blood-related.

Grandpaw and Uncle Lee always spoke about history. Uncle Lee's son, James was just like me, we both loved family history. I sleep and breathe our family history, I think of it all the time because when I was coming up, they talked about it all the time. I have tried to teach y'all about the family history because you can't let us die. If I do not tell the story, it will be all over with and a lot of folks may think they know us, but listen to me because I know what I am talking about.

Let me get back to Bibb County. Ma Lide told the family about our Uncle Rupel – look him up for yourself. Rupel Avery left Bibb County and headed North to become free because he was tired of slavery. Some white folks were involved with helping him go North. Once Uncle Rupel left Bibb County, no one saw him again, but somebody told the slaves he was safe and okay.

I always said I should have named one of my sons, Rupel. That name always stayed with me because I never heard of anyone named Rupel. Uncle Lee and Grandpaw also spoke about Moses Avery. Uncle Moses' was connected to Ma Lide's side. Double-check me, but I think it was first Uncle Moses' family that moved to Mississippi.

Today, I still deal with all the folks that I know of from Mississippi that are connected to the Avery side. All of Uncle Tommy McWilliams' children still live in Drew, MS and Ruleville, MS. The McWilliams once lived in Rushing Spring. They always come back home to visit me and they never miss an Avery funeral. I had all of them to come home to Rushing Spring when we built our new church.

We were with our Grandpaw just about every day since all of us lived in Rushing Spring, but Uncle Lee lived on Ketona Road before he moved to Pine Hill Road in Ketona. So really Uncle Lee was right down the street from us. Grandpaw was softer with his words than Uncle Lee. Uncle Lee did not care how he said things – he just said it and he was more talkative than Grandpaw.

Uncle Lee always bossed Grandpaw and told him what to do. Grandpaw did not go against Uncle Lee. My Uncle Lee was a big talker and do not try to prove him wrong because you would not win. Grandpaw was a preacher so that may have influenced how he treated folks. I will say they both loved God and in my head right now, I can hear them singing while working in the fields.

They both had odd jobs and at one point they worked as janitors at the courthouse. When they got off work, we worked in the fields with them growing vegetables and tending our animals. As they got older, they just gave us orders while working in the fields. Both of them had bad knees.

Grandpaw and Uncle Lee told us about how they had to leave Bibb County as boys. They left their running! Slavery was over with by law when they left, but the slave master still tried to hold on to his former slaves and their children. The former slaves still had to work under their slave master to survive.

When slavery ended, Grandpaw told us that slaves could not move too far from the slave master and they still had to report to the slave master. The white Avery's owned us probably one hundred years or it may have even been two hundred years. Grandpaw would say, "I know good white folks and bad white folks, just like I know good black folks and bad black folks."

They told us that whites and blacks worked together in the fields down in Bibb County, but the blacks received the worse treatment. Since Grandpaw and Uncle Lee were young boys, the white folks worked them all day and night because they were fast workers. They were given no freedom and had to work like they were still in slavery. Somebody down there started treating them real bad and they decided it was time to get the hell out of there. They talked with their mother and she agreed. They told us about a man called 'Ole Man Seth'. This man was not their father, but he was a strong father figure. They loved 'Ole Man Seth'. I don't know for sure, but I do not think he was a relative, but he encouraged them to get out of Bibb County and they always talked about him. Now if they did something illegal down there as boys, they never told us about it, but Grandpaw told us once he left Bibb County, he could not tell anyone the truth about his name and age. He lied about his age even up until he died.

I can remember asking both of them how they got away from Bibb County because you could tell they did not like that place. I never like to use the word hate, but I think they hated that place.

Grandpaw told us how they had to run to the train track and jump on and off the train. They knew the train would carry them out of Bibb County. The whole family was ready to get away from there, but that slave master tried to hold on to them as long as he could. This is one thing I remember he said, "Whannie, we rode the train at night and had to be real quiet. We jumped on that train together and would jump off that train together." I remember him saying that the white folks would have killed them if they had been caught. As I said, slavery was over, but some of them still got in trouble if they were not around to work.

I just remembered, Grandpaw told us about when they were jumping off the train, sometimes they had to hide in fields and he would put his hair over their faces so that no one would see them. He said they had to be so quiet until both he and Uncle Lee could read each other's body language without talking. He told many stories about how they preferred to ride the trains at night because the darkness blended in with their skin.

When I was growing up, Grandpaw had really long, straight, black hair that went past his belt. Although he and Uncle Lee said their daddy was Alexander Avery, I always wondered why Grandpaw's hair was different from Uncle Lee's hair. I wondered if they really had the same daddy. I know it may not mean anything, but Uncle Lee's hair was short and very coarse. They both had the same brown skin tone.

There did come a point when Grandpaw and Uncle Lee had to split up while jumping on and off the train. All I know is when they split up Grandpaw came toward this way where we live, but he made a few stops before reaching Tarrant City. There were times he had to live as a boarder with various families. Uncle Lee told us, but I cannot remember where Uncle Lee went before coming to Tarrant.

GRANDPAW'S LIFE CHANGED when he met the Goins' family from Rushing Spring. Alexander and Hannah Goins were former slaves and well-known because they had a lot of land. The Goins helped former slaves get on their feet by giving them somewhere to sleep, work and eat. Rushing Spring was really a safe haven for freed slaves. Grandpaw said the Goins would even let Blacks come there to rest for a few days before moving on to a different town. They believed in helping people.

I gave Charles Jr. the papers on Rushing Spring. Go look at the papers, you will see where it says Alexander Goins obtained the property we call Rushing Spring on May 12, 1885 – look at the first page. The papers I gave Charles Jr. have been around since the 1800s so if the house catches fire, grab the papers, then y'all run [chuckling]!

Grandpaw called Alexander Goins "Ole Man Goins". Alexander Goins was a preacher when Grandpaw met him. Grandpaw went to him for work, food, and shelter. He told us that Alexander Goins was short, but when he opened his mouth, he was a powerhouse and everybody listened. You see Alexander Goins was a preacher and my Grandpaw eventually became a preacher.

Alexander Goins was married to Hannah Goins and they had four children. I believe it was two of the children died young, but Simon Goins and Jenny Goins lived into adulthood. Grandpaw ended up marrying Jenny Goins. We called Jenny Goins, "Grandmaw". Grandmaw gave birth to Levi, Hannah, Rector Alexander, Nannie, Pearl, Shepherd, and Jessie Mae. I think I named all of them – double-check me again.

Uncle Shep was the youngest son and he married Aunt Lena. Uncle Shep and Aunt Lena never had kids. Aunt Lena was light brown, real thin, but so nice to everybody. She loved to surprise us with gifts. Uncle Shep became the Associate Pastor at Rushing Spring.

Aunt Jessie Mae married a man named Jesse Scott, whom we called "Coloreda" because he served time in the Colorado prison. While in prison, he was on the chain gang and he would drag his leg when he walked because he was so use to pulling that chain on his leg. Being in prison, really messed up his mind because he was ready to fight or shoot at anything. If the wind was blowing too hard or if the leaves rustled, Coloreda may start shooting because he thought someone was after him.

Aunt Nannie never had kids. Her first husband was Vann Orr. Vann got into trouble and Aunt Nannie's second husband was John Barnes. Uncle John was a short, sanctified preacher and always wore black, rubber boots. He would wear those rubber boots even when he wore his black, Sunday suit. Uncle John was full of the Holy Ghost. When he preached, he loved jumping up and down. He would get so happy in the Spirit and would dance all over the church.

When he was not preaching, Uncle John taught us how to train dogs and we sometimes hunted with him. He had a lot of dogs and even trained dogs for the white men in the area. My brothers and I enjoyed helping Uncle John.

Uncle Levi was also married to a lady named Jennie. Aunt Jennie's maiden name might have been Latham. Nobody from Ketona can ever forget Uncle Levi. He would walk around with two sticks because he was so old. That man was still walking from Rushing Spring to Ketona even in his old age. Uncle Levi's kids were Clara and Felix. Felix was married to Velma and then Mattie. Felix was never really active in church and I do not know why he was not because his wife, Velma was a Sunday School Teacher at Rushing Spring. When he and Velma split up, he married Mattie, who was a nurse at the Jefferson County Nursing Home. Mattie took care of a lot of folks in Ketona.

Uncle Lee's daughter, Mattie Pearl was named after Aunt Pearl. Aunt Pearl did not live long. I never heard a whole lot about the daughter named Hannah, who was named after Grandmaw's mother. Wait, we had a lady in Rushing Spring, we called Aunt Bell and her house stayed up there for a long time. I was grown and that house was still there.

Now, go in my folder and you will see the signatures of a lot of the folks I am naming. All of them had to sign papers to give the church some extra land and I kept a copy since it was history.

Grandmaw's brother was Simon Goins and he married Ella. Simon's real name was Joe Simon, but he just used Simon. Ella was from Georgia and they had a daughter named Nannie Lee Goins. As you can see, Nannie is also a popular name in the family. Uncle Simon lived in Rushing Spring too. After his wife Ella died, he married a lady named Lizzie.

LET ME TELL YOU ABOUT GRANDMAW. She was a frail, sickly woman. She was skinny and not tall. She kept her head covered up, I guess, so she would not catch a cold. Now, I think she was always sick because she had too many babies. Grandmaw was too small to have all those babies, just too puny—now that's just me talking.

I remember my Aunts, Uncles, even my father crying when Grandmaw would get sick because no one knew when death was coming for her. Grandpaw was always overprotective of her. As a child, we saw Grandpaw show love to Grandmaw – that was the norm. He would hold her and be so nice. He talked softly to her.

A lot of men back then did not show that much affection, but Grandpaw did. She did not have to do much around the house because he did a lot and all of the children helped. Grandpaw would lean over her and pray. Grandpaw was always singing Grandmaw had a little voice too – she could sing soprano. She taught us a song about a rabbit – I guess you would call them nursery rhymes. All of us would sing up at their house. She loved it. When we went to their house, we always sat around her bed and no one cut up either, we knew her health condition.

Grandmaw never had anything to worry about and she stayed in bed a lot. I can see her now in bed with her quilt looking at us just smiling. She was a nice lady, really nice lady. She wanted us to do our work in school and she did not play about school. When she spoke it was always really soft and we made her happy. When she wasn't sick, she could cook anything. Grandpaw would bathe her and we would help get the spring water to be boiled for her bath water. Grandpaw would help her get dressed and sometimes he had to even feed her because she was too weak. Really, when you think about it, Grandpaw was teaching all of us how to treat a woman in sickness and in health and for better or worse.

When you are driving up to Rushing Spring, my grandparents lived up in the cut to your right. No, they did not have a big house; you know it was a small house made of all wood. I do not remember whether that house was painted on the inside or the outside. I remember the floor had no carpet, it had wooden planks. You ought to remember that house because it sat there a long time, way after they died. Now a lot of folks stayed in that house with my grandparents.

Near the front porch of my grandparents' home were fruit trees. Grandpaw always took naps on his porch with his feet propped up on the wooden railing. When he would go to sleep, we called ourselves sneaking to take the fruit off one of the trees. All of us climbed trees back then. We could not pass a fast one on him because he always woke up and said "Y'all leave that tree alone!" Grandpaw never hit us, but he would speak firm to us when needed.

Now my Grandmaw did not like to be around Uncle Lee. Grandmaw could not stand the sight of Uncle Lee. She did not encourage any of us to be around him outside of work. It was said that Uncle Lee was very rude with his words to Grandmaw and said something about her appearance. Since I always helped Uncle Lee and Grandpaw in the fields, I heard probably more than I should have heard.

Despite Grandmaw not liking Uncle Lee, Grandpaw and Uncle Lee always worked together. Uncle Lee did not ever go inside my grandparents' home because of my Grandmaw. Even right now, there is sort of a slight split between Grandpaw's children and Uncle's Lee's children because Grandmaw did not want us to deal with Uncle Lee. You would not know that some of us are family. Those old folks have been dead for almost one hundred years and the split in the family still exists. We ain't never sat at the dinner table with Uncle Lee's family at one time. As years passed, my children formed a relationship with Uncle Lee's grandchildren because of playing together and going to school together.

MY UNCLE LEE DID NOT GO to church with us, but his wife did after he died. Uncle Lee went to church over in Zion City. Before there was Rushing Spring Baptist Church, most of the family attended church in Zion City. Even my mama's family, the Woods, went to church in Zion City.

Alexander Goins along with other families from Ketona eventually started a prayer band. They would go house to house praying and having church. Then, they started having church under a brush harbor. Later, they named their place of worship "Goins Chapel" and since that sounded like a Methodist church and they were Baptist, they changed the name to Rushing Spring Baptist Church. The church is named after all the springs over there. They did not start the church until 1891. Grandpaw and Ole Man Goins were preachers, but they did not want to serve as the Pastor of the church because they were not good at reading and writing. Look at the papers I gave your daddy, back then they signed everything with the letter "X."

Grandpaw said he and Ole Man Goins put in place the first rule of the church that whoever would Pastor the church had to be somewhat literate and really know the Bible. I always said that shows they were humble men and knew their limitations because they could have easily served as the Pastor.

WAIT, AS I AM TALKING, I CAN REMEMBER when I was a boy, all of us, one Sunday were sitting in church. I was sitting to the left of the church, next to my Grandmaw. A white man with a black suit walked in and said, "Is Alexander Avery in here?"

Grandmaw held on to my knee and as a child, I could tell something ain't right. Papa stood up and said, "I am Rector Alexander Avery." The white man asked his age and Papa responded. The white man then said, "I know it is an Alexander Avery somewhere around here." My Grandpaw did not open his mouth, but at that point, I had no idea his real name was Alexander Avery.

By the time Uncle Lee got out of church, somebody had to tell him what happened at church because that was the first and only time I saw

Uncle Lee run up that hill to Grandpaw. Uncle Levi was standing near the house with a shotgun and Papa cried. As I grew older, I asked Grandpaw about it because he talked to me about a lot, but he played like he had amnesia and never told me why that white man came to Rushing Spring. As I grew older, I wondered if that white man was from Bibb County because not too many people knew Grandpaw's real name was Alexander.

Grandpaw and Uncle Lee did not agree on everything, but when it was time to stand together, they did it. I will say that Grandpaw and Uncle Lee loved their sisters and their sisters' children. Let me think, some of the sisters' names were Lucinda [Cindy], Malinda, Lucretia, and Maria. Aunt Cindy Hardy's house was in Jonesboro down in Bessemer, Alabama. Aunt Cindy died when I was really young, but the family still remained close and we always visited. Although Aunt Cindy was dead, the family always shared stories about her. All of us got excited when it was time to go to Jonesboro because when we got to the house, it was packed with family and a lot of food. Charles Jr. can show you the house because it is still there.

Whenever the older Avery's got sick and about to die, they went to Jonesboro down to my Aunt's house. They had to stay there until they died. After Aunt Cindy died, her daughters cared for all the older Avery's.

You know the older cousins down there still called me until they died and when they died I lost touch with a lot of our folks on the Hardy and Mayfield side. I remember when Aunt Cindy's side had funerals because we, Avery's would attend the funerals. Back then, we tried to attend everything they had going on down there if we knew about it. As we grew older, some of them would call my sister, Senie and she would round us up to go down to Jonesboro.

One of my cousins from Jonesboro was Minnie Hardy Mayfield and I knew her children. When we had funerals at Rushing Spring, our folks from Jonesboro would come and spend the day with us.

I WAS A BOY, but I can remember the day Grandmaw died. Our folks from Jonesboro came to be with us. We could not control Grandpaw because he was full of tears. It was a sad day, really sad day. It was said that Grandpaw was probably the first black in our area that ordered a metal casket. He wanted Grandmaw to have the best. I remember people talking and making a big deal about Grandmaw's casket.

Everybody was crowded around her casket, just crying, even me. The whites in the area could not understand how Grandpaw could afford a metal casket and he was questioned about that metal casket. After we buried her, some of the whites went walking on our property with a metal detector; they were looking for gold and dug up my Grandmaw's grave! They dug her up and threw her out of the casket and they left her there hanging out of the CASKET! We did not know someone disturbed her grave until somebody walked up there. Once Grandpaw found out he was mad as hell. I can see him now squinting his eyes and biting his lip. He grabbed his shotgun, ready to fight. He was mad! When you go up to the grave, you will see a flat concrete slab over Grandmaw's grave; we did that after they dug her up. It was a white man that told Grandpaw about the metal detector incident.

When Grandpaw became sick, he was taken to Jonesboro and Uncle Lee was with him. We visited with him. I remember Uncle Lee wiped his face with a towel. Uncle Lee sat by his bed. After he died, they brought

Grandpaw's body back to Rushing Spring. Uncle Lee helped plan Grandpaw's funeral and I was there in the room with everybody. The family planned the funeral while sitting at the dining table where I grew up. When they were planning the funeral, that's how I learned about Grandpaw's real age, Uncle Lee explained it to us. My Uncle Lee loved Grandpaw and he tried to stay strong, but you could see that he was hurting. On that day, Grandpaw's children did exactly what Uncle Lee said and nobody had a disagreement. Grandpaw is buried next to Grandmaw and he too has a concrete slab over his burial site. They are both buried at our cemetery on top of the hill.

Grandpaw was our world and I still feel his spirit. My grandfather was a big dreamer and yeah, he taught us all to dream. To have no formal education, he and Grandmaw instilled education in all of us. They taught us that we can do anything we wanted to do. Grandpaw was big on spending time with all of his children and grandchildren. I can't say anything bad about him because baby, he was good to us. He could farm, he could cook, preach, sing and he prayed all the time. I can hear him now praying for all of us. He would holler and clap his hands saying, "Ohhhhhh Lord, my God, we thank you!"

Chapter 4

Brewster & Turnbow

I BECAME INTERESTED in Eula Clyde Brewster Avery in the late 1930s. It is ironic, but we shared the same first cousin, Percy "Buddy" Turnbow. Buddy was the son to Eula's Uncle Chrisell, who was her mother's brother. Buddy was also the son to my mother's sister, Charlottie. I always thought that was a rare coincidence.

However, Eula caught my eye because she had some meat on her bones and she was tough. Eula did not bite her tongue for anyone. Eula was crazy about me and did not play about when it came to me and my family. I called her "Doll Heart" and she called me "Daddy".

We married on September 15, 1940, after church service. Eula was nineteen and I had to be around twenty-three years old. We married on the front porch at my home in Rushing Spring. My brother, Rec officiated the wedding service. I wore a black suit with black shoes and Eula wore a blue dress with black shoes. Our oldest son, Tom was in her arms during the wedding ceremony and then he reached for me.

Mama had flowers all over the front porch on our wedding day. Our parents along with our siblings attended the wedding ceremony. A few church members and other family members were there supporting us. Before the wedding, Aunt Lozzie and my sisters took me in my bedroom to make sure I was ready to leave home. I told them, "Y'all, I will just be down the street in Ketona. I will be fine. Nothing will change." You know how sisters are, but I went ahead and did what my heart told me to do.

After the wedding, we moved into Eula's childhood home with Mama Jenny, Papa Murray, and Aunt Josie Hardy. For a wedding gift, my parents bought us brand new bedroom furniture, white bed linens, white blanket and gave us ten, one-dollar bills. Ten dollars was a lot of money back then. Papa said, "Hold on to that money." On our wedding night, we slept in our new bed with our oldest son. Right now, my wedding gift from my parents still looks brand new and sits in my middle bedroom. When you spend a little money and buy real wood, it will last a long time.

MY WIFE'S FATHER was Aaron Brewster from Village Springs near Pinson, Alabama. I remember them saying his mother's name was Margaret Brewster from Rome, Georgia. His father's name was either Edward or Edwin and he was from Tennessee. Whenever you meet someone and their last name is Murphy, Hamby or Fomby and their roots are from Village Springs, they are relatives of Aaron Brewster. Some of his sisters or maybe it was one sister married into the Murphy family. The Hamby and Fomby families from Village Springs are the children of Mr. Aaron's siblings.

I met Mr. Aaron as a young child and I had no idea that one day I would marry his daughter. He was short, dark brown, silky, black hair and always wore work clothes. Mr. Aaron was known for singing Negro spirituals. His nephew, Ruphus Murphy from Village Springs lived in Ketona with Mama Jenny and Mr. Aaron. I remember playing in Ketona and Mr. Aaron taught us how to throw a baseball. He took turns with each one of us until we got it right.

Mama Jenny also came from Village Springs. Mama Jenny's family was made up of Cherokee Indians. Her parents were Lewis and Elizabeth Turnbow. Elizabeth Turnbow's mother was Minnie Cornelius. Mama Jenny told us stories about how her forefathers came from out West and migrated to Alabama. Mama Jenny's full name was Jenny Elizabeth Turnbow Brewster Murray. The names of her siblings that I can remember are Sara, Della "Dude", Raymond, Jackson, Arthur, Chrisell, Buddy "Bud" and Minnie. Uncle Bud was the youngest brother and Minnie was the youngest sister. Whenever Mama Jenny spoke of family history, I tried to remember what she was saying and Eula would write it down in the family Bible. Check with Charles Jr. to find out, who has that Bible because it has a lot of these names. This is another example of why this book must be published – write everything down!

When some of Mama Jenny's family moved up North, they changed the spelling of their last name to T-U-R-N-B-O. Uncle Bud's children live in Illinois and Nevada and they use the spelling, T-U-R-N-B-O. My children keep up with all of Uncle Bud's children. Uncle Chrisell's descendants that I know of are here in Alabama, Tennessee, and Maryland. Out of Uncle Chrisell's grandchildren, we hear from Carl and Pervis and when Percy Lee and Gwen were living, they always stopped and would sit in the living room to catch up with us. Aunt Della's descendants moved to Michigan and keep in touch with my daughters.

When Mr. Aaron and Mama Jenny left Village Springs, they lived near Murphy Road in Ketona. Their home was near water and often flooded. Before Mr. Aaron died, they built the home across the train tracks located at 729 Pine Hill Road. When you jump those train tracks, this is the first house you will see. He built this home large enough for his growing family.

Mr. Aaron was a driller for the Ketona Rock Quarry. TCI owned the rock quarry. The rock quarry is home to two of the largest lakes known as Ketona Lakes. The bottom of the lakes still holds equipment used by former rock quarry workers. Several people drowned in this lake. Back then, people would try to swim across the lakes and many did not make it. Napoleon Embry, Sr. was always successful in swimming across the lake. Everybody would watch him swim. I could swim, but I did not want to take a chance of losing my life because that water is deep.

Mr. Aaron died while blasting rock down in the Ketona Rock Quarry in 1927. While he was drilling one morning, rocks became loose and a rock hit him in the head. When he fell down, all of the small rocks came down and crushed him while down in the rock quarry.

The rock quarry was not far from his home located at 729 Pine Hill Road. Once the workers saw him dead, they ran to get Mama Jenny. Mama Jenny and all of her children ran down to the rock quarry and saw him dead. The workers along with his sons pulled Mr. Aaron from up under the rocks. Mama Jenny told stories of how she laid on top of his body before his body was taken away. She kissed him and did not want to let him go. Her boys pulled her away from his body. She said although her boys were very young when their father died, on that day they became men.

Before she went back home, Mama Jenny removed all of Mr. Aaron's belongings from his pocket and took off his Mason ring. She wrapped his items with her handkerchief and kept them inside this house.

When Mama Jenny died, Eula put Mr. Aaron's items in a safe place because she did not want anyone to bother his belongings. After Eula died, in 1989, I gave everything to Charles Jr. and told him to keep everything in a safe place. When Charles Jr. shows you Mr. Aaron's belongings, you will see that Mama Jenny's handkerchief still has the dirt from the rock quarry. Please, take care of his belongings – this is history.

As a result of Mr. Aaron's death, the Ketona Rock Quarry gave all his sons jobs. They all accepted the jobs to help Mama Jenny survive. TCI later relocated Mama Jenny's sons to Bessemer, Alabama. This is why all them ended up living in Bessemer in the Jonesboro neighborhood.

MY WIFE'S FIRST COUSIN, whom she loved like a sister is our Aunt Bessie. Aunt Bessie has a very long name and I hope I can remember all of it. Her full name is Bessie Vessie Elizabeth Virginia Turnbow Price. All of us call her Aunt Bessie or Sis. Price. Aunt Bessie's mother was Minnie Turnbow, the younger sister of my mother-in-law, Mama Jenny.

Aunt Bessie was born in Village Springs, Alabama and her mother died while giving birth to her. As a result, Minnie's older sister, Sara raised her during the school months and Aunt Bessie spent the summer months with Mama Jenny in Ketona. The Turnbow family felt it was best for Aunt Sara to raise Aunt Bessie since she only had one son in her home. Sometimes

Aunt Sara would write Aunt Bessie's name as Bessie Turnbow Miller because Aunt Sara was once married to a Miller.

Aunt Sara left Village Springs and relocated to Chattanooga, TN. Aunt Sara had more than one husband and one of those husbands, Aunt Bessie still cannot stand. Today, Aunt Bessie has dementia, but she still speaks about how mean Aunt Sara's husband was to them. Now, the husband she is speaking about, I do not know, she just says, "Mama's husband was a mean, low down man to us." He must have done something awful for that to still be on her conscious.

Even though I am blind, I made a promise to my wife that I would take care of Aunt Bessie. Eula died on January 6, 1989, and Aunt Bessie still lives in the front bedroom. I am thankful that my children here in town help me take care of Aunt Bessie and Jerri is the primary caretaker.

When Aunt Bessie became grown, she married John W. Price. Aunt Bessie and John co-owned a grocery store in Chattanooga, TN known as Price Brothers Grocery. Aunt Bessie served as the bookkeeper. Aunt Sara was a big fan of John because he could give Aunt Bessie a better life and he did just that. John and Aunt Bessie were always well-off financially and he would drive her to Ketona and Chattanooga every year to visit family.

When they visited Ketona, they stayed here with us. Aunt Bessie would always call ahead of time to let us know when she was coming. Eula would get on the telephone and tell everyone from Ketona, Village Springs and Bessemer, Aunt Bessie's arrival date. When Aunt Bessie and John were in town, our front door would be swinging back and forth with the company. It is a blessing when people love you and want to come see you. Aunt Bessie's favorite visitor would be Uncle Chrisell Turnbow. When she saw her Uncle Chrisell, she was like a little kid at Christmas time. Uncle Chrisell would step on the porch saying, "Where is my niece?" When Aunt Bessie heard his voice, she would run to that porch saying, "Uncle Chrisell, Uncle Chrisell!" They would hug for a long time.

I am sure she reminded him of his sister, Minnie. Uncle Chrisell helped both Sara and Mama Jenny financially with Bessie's care when she was a child. One time, Uncle Chrisell told John, "Treat her right or Bessie is coming home." Every time, Uncle Chrisell sat at our kitchen table, one of his favorite sayings to Eula was, "Niecy, it's good to be here where nobody ain't throwing bricks!" Uncle Chrisell was so much fun and we loved for him to joke with us.

Now in your lifetime, you never saw Aunt Bessie drive a car, but she could drive. Then one day, she suddenly stopped driving. Aunt Sara was killed in a car accident and that messed Aunt Bessie up mentally and Aunt Bessie said, "I will never drive again." The car accident occurred because the driver fell asleep and hit a tree. Aunt Sara was thrown out of the car and broke her neck because she did not have a seat belt on. When Aunt Sara died, her last name was Davis.

After leaving Chattanooga, John and Aunt Bessie relocated to Chicago. John retired from the Post Office and Aunt Bessie retired from Mercy Hospital. John and Aunt Bessie never had children, but she was close to most of her younger cousins. Really, Aunt Bessie did not have any nieces and nephews because she was Minnie's only child.

When John died in the 1980s, Eula convinced Aunt Bessie to leave Chicago and relocate to Ketona. Eula did not want Aunt Bessie living by herself. During that time, Aunt Bessie had a white, large dog named

Pinoco. When Eula said, "Sis. Price needs to be with us so she will not be by herself." I had no problem with Aunt Bessie coming to live here, but I honestly did not want another dog. Soon after Aunt Bessie agreed to relocate with us, the dog died.

Eula went to Chicago and stayed one month to pack Aunt Bessie's home. When she came back, Uncle Roy rented a U-Haul. My son, Charles Jr. and grandsons, Chuck, Tommy and Gregory helped us move Aunt Bessie to Birmingham. When we arrived back to Ketona, Uncle Chrisell and Skeet were sitting on the front porch ready to work. Pete, my brother-in-law, came to Ketona from Chicago to help us get the house ready for Aunt Bessie.

When we got back from Chicago, a decision had to be made on our dining room table in Ketona. It was special because it had always been in the family. No one had room for it and Eula said to her brother, "Roy, go ahead and get rid of it." Eula left the room and Roy took an ax and tore it into pieces. We then took the pieces outback and burned it. After doing that, we moved in Aunt Bessie's dining room furniture. I know the table we got rid of was special to Eula because, for decades, anyone that was an Avery Turnbow or Brewster spent a lot of time at that dining room table.

Ester Brewster Williams

"Go to Esther and her girls. I want them to speak on behalf of the Brewster side of the family because Uncle Jack and his kids spent a lot of time here with us. Uncle Jack called every morning. Eula was crazy about all of Jack's children." – Charles D. Avery, Sr.

SOME CALL ME ESTHER MAE OR ESTHER RUTH and I have one huge family. I am the daughter of James "Jack" Benjamin Brewster, who was married to my mother, Della Cornelius Robinson Brewster. My parents died a few months apart in the 1970s. My father's parents are Aaron Brewster and Mama Jenny. My brothers are Fletcher Moss, James "Jack" Brewster, Jr., Charles Brewster, Robert Brewster, and the youngest brother is Willie Brewster. My brother, Jack will always be known for playing baseball for the Birmingham Black Barons. My sisters are Dianna "Diane" McMillan, Shirley Williams and youngest sister is Teresia Brewster. Our father worked for TCI U.S. Steel in Bessemer, AL.

We lived at Route 8, Box #855 down in Jonesboro located in Bessemer. Our home was painted white and inside we had three bedrooms, two bathrooms along with a living room, dining room, and kitchen. Since I had so many sisters and brothers, my Uncle Roy and Uncle Skeet helped my parents financially. My uncles would bring food to our home and drove us around when needed. I do not recall seeing Daddy drive a car. Daddy's sister, Aunt Olivia, who lived in Chicago provided us clothes to wear.

When customers would not pick up their clothes from the dry cleaners where she worked, she mailed them to us.

Daddy, Uncle Roy and Uncle Skeet were strong deacons at our church, St. Paul CME Church down in Bessemer. These three brothers were spiritual and all of us went to church with them. Daddy and his brothers always stuck together and they treated everyone with love and kindness

We all grew up spending time at 729 Pine Hill Road because we called it the "home house". I can see Aunt Eula now standing on the front porch waiting on us to all get out of the car. When we walked up to the steps, she made it a point to hug and kiss each one of us when we entered her home and when we left. When we entered the house, Uncle Charles and our cousins would greet us with hugs. All of the children, including Aunt Eula's children, gathered in the kitchen and dining room to eat hotdogs with sauerkraut. When we finished eating, we rushed to the backyard to watch the ducks in their pond. Our grandmother, Mama Jenny would be sitting there in the kitchen and was glad to see us. Mama Jenny would have a huge smile when Daddy walked thru the door. When Daddy walked thru the door, he yelled, "Mama, I am home!" A lot of times Uncle Roy and Uncle Skeet would be there with us. The home house at 729 Pine Hill Road could hold a lot of people.

Mama Jenny did not play! Our brother, Willie was still on a bottle at the age of three. Mama Jenny took that bottle from him and threw it down the train track. I became angry at her, but I did not let her know it because Mama Jenny would pop you with the wood handle of her butter knife. All of us knew that we better not cut up with her. One fun thing, she would let us do was bang on the piano in the living room. Everyone took turns banging on that piano making tons of noise.

Daddy felt Ketona was just like heaven. While we were with Aunt Eula, Daddy went house-to-house visiting everyone in Ketona. We could hear the voices of Daddy, Uncle Roy and Uncle Skeet joyfully greeting people outside. Daddy had a way of giving everyone nicknames. He called Charles Jr, 'Shalaki'.

Daddy spoiled all of his kids rotten and anyone will tell you that I will always be a Daddy's girl. My Uncle Charles, Aunt Eula, Aunt Olivia, and Uncle Pete were very special to me. My sister, Diane looks just like Aunt Eula's daughter, Dot. They could pass for sisters. Charles Jr. and I have always been close, I have his back and he has my back – always!

I have two daughters, Kenna and Jai. Daddy called Kenna, "Jack Rabbit" and Jai, "Shaku"; we will never know how he came up with his nicknames. Each morning before school, he called my girls singing an old folklore. The girls looked forward to his phone call every single morning. I remember Daddy taking time with Diane's boys to show them how to play marbles.

I raised my girls in the Northside Housing Projects in Bessemer. Daddy and my family helped me raise my girls. Back then, families stuck together. My girls knew they never had anything to worry about because Daddy and his brothers would always help.

I left Bessemer in the 1960s due to my husband's military duties at Fort McClellan. Later, in the 1970s, my girls and I relocated to Boston, MA. After spending a few years in Boston, Aunt Olivia and Uncle Pete convinced me to move to Chicago, IL. Years later, Uncle Charles was the one who said, "Esther, you need to be closer to home." After hearing words of wisdom, I felt it was the right thing to do by relocating to Georgia with my daughter, Jai.

Kenna & Jai

I TELL KENNA that I am thankful for family. We grew up knowing love and receiving love. Love runs all through me because of my foundation. Just like Mama mentioned, Aunt Eula showered them with love when they arrived at her home, she did the same thing for us. Now in my own home, I make it a point to shower my guests with hugs and love.

My sister, Jai will agree to the point that our foundation provided the groundwork for our spirituality and prayer life. We grew up around family, who shared a love for God and they worked for God. We grew up with family showing us, it is a joy to serve God. Even today, when we go to Rushing Spring to see family, we feel right at home. A lot of family members have gone on to be with the Lord, but Mama, Jai and I are thankful that the Brewster family left their mark in Jonesboro down in Bessemer and no one will forget our family from Ketona right there by the train track in Tarrant City

PART 2
OUR COMMUNITY

Chapter 5

———————

Thankful

"Make sure you speak to James "Bubba" & Lucinda's kids. Our families
have been together way over one hundred years. I want their kids and all
Avery's to stick together. You will need each other."
— Charles D. Avery, Sr.

Darryl Sankey

I FIRST STARTED ATTENDING Rushing Spring Baptist Church after
I was born. I have been part of the church family for over forty years.
When I think of Rushing Spring, the first thing that comes to my mind is
my Granddad. He made sure his grandkids received a strong spiritual
foundation. Back in the 1980s, most of us grandkids either lived in Gate
City or Collegeville – that's about 15 minutes from Rushing Spring.

Sunday School started at 9:00 am and Granddad left the house at 7:45

am to make his rounds to pick us up. When Granddad arrived to our homes, we were all dressed and ready to go because we started getting our clothes ready for church on Saturday. Granddad was dressed with his Sunday best and we were too. Inside the station wagon was Puddin, Fred, Eric, Trice, Jessica, Scoob and your truly sitting in total silence. The only noise you would hear was WATV gospel radio with Rev. Fausch.

Once we hit Highway 79 to go into Ketona, the car wheels jumped the train tracks, and the car would shake. Next, we drove down Pine Hill Road and turned left onto Rushing Spring Road. Once we saw Rushing Spring Road, everyone got excited because Rushing Spring Baptist Church was and still is, the place to be! It was exciting because we were with all of our family and close friends.

Rushing Spring Baptist Church is where my Granddad grew up. My Granddad's grandparents went to Rushing Spring along with his parents, then Granddad's generation, then Granddad's children, his grandkids, now his great-grandkids and great-great grandkids. That is a total of seven generations that I know of that met Jesus right there on the hill at Rushing Spring. All we know is Rushing Spring; it is embedded in all of us.

Once we got out of the car on Sundays, with Granddad, all the boys had to help get two orange, plastic water coolers out of the trunk of the car. While we were doing that, Granddad unlocked the church door. Once he unlocked the door, we walked into church as a family with Granddad leading us. Since the church did not have city water, Granddad always ensured, the members had cool water to drink. One water cooler was placed on a small table in the hallway and the back-up cooler went to the kitchen. Small, paper cups were placed next to the water cooler table.

Before the start of Sunday School, Granddad would pull out his black coin purse from his side pocket and give us money to put into the offering collection plate for Sunday School. After we received our money, we sat quietly in the sanctuary until the others arrived. Whenever, we heard the church door open, our heads would turn to see, who was coming. When our friends and family arrived, there were no sad faces, everybody was happy. Everybody greeted each other. Most of the Deacons would arrive first before anyone, then, everybody else would come in. Right now in my mind, I can see Brother J.T. Byrd leading his family in, then Uncle Joe, the Avery's, Brother Julius Brown, Brother Jesse Peterson and so many others. We had men that were workers and leaders.

Back then, Sunday School was overflowing with kids because our parents and grandparents did not give us an option. Sunday was a special, sacred time and we were taught to take it seriously. You automatically knew that you were going to Sunday School even if you had been busy with school activities. All of us loved our Sunday School teachers and they loved us. Sister Prentella Brown was a Sunday School teacher that stood out along with her daughter, Sister Maxine Brown. They both were virtuous women and very soft-spoken. Every child brought up at Rushing Spring knows the Word of God. Sister Maxine Brown now teaches my nephews; she is serious about the Holy Bible.

In addition to teaching us about God, the church helped to develop our social skills and taught us the importance of family. We always address our church family as sisters and brothers. All of us were taught how to respect our elders. Everyone raised in Rushing Spring will always protect and love each other because we are one family. Even if we get mad at each other, we will still see about each other. When families have been together over one hundred years, I do not care what happens, they will come back together because you cannot break the bond that has existed for so many generations.

Wait, listen to this, my favorite part of church was to hear Sister Sue Embry sing the song, "Surely" – Lord she could sing that song! Oh Lord, just to think about it right now, gives me chills and makes me clap my hands because when she started singing, she was preaching to us. When Sister Sue grabbed the microphone, we would just stop what we were doing because we were about to have a *little church*! Sister Jerri Avery would be on the piano with that arch in her back looking down at the keys and Brother Singleton Lewis would be on the organ looking at Sue because they knew they had to play that song and give it their all.

When Sister Sue sang the first word of the song, the entire church would double clap and stand on their feet, even the kids. Everybody knew how to do our double clap from the youngest to the oldest. Then it is a part in the song where she was so into the song, she would stomp her foot and then put her hand on her hip and forcefully say, "Don't you know God is able?" When she asked that, it was like a mother telling a child, "Don't touch that hot stove or look both ways before you cross the street." Sister Sue was teaching us God is able!

While she was singing, the church went wild, even us as kids felt the Holy Ghost! Now don't let it be a Sunday where Sister Maxine Brown came behind Sister Sue and start singing "God Specializes" – nobody can sing that song like her! When Sister Maxine starts off that song, she closes her eyes because she has to get in tune with the Holy Ghost. She never opens her eyes because she goes to another spiritual level and we go there with her. Then, Sister Maxine will even hunch her shoulders and start off slowly saying the words, "God Specializes" and she takes her time singing it. When she sings the first two lyrics, it is all over. Folks start falling out, shouting and smiling because the Holy Ghost is all over Rushing Spring. Whenever the Holy Ghost stops by Rushing Spring, I have even heard that Ebenezer Baptist in Ketona is on Holy Ghost fire. It is a part in the Sister Maxine's song when the tenors come behind the ladies and say, "God specializes," even the male children in the congregation would join in with our tenors, Granddad, Brother Avery, Brother Booker, and Brother Byrd.

All youth from my generation received the best voice training. We all know how to not just sing words, but we were taught the meaning of the words. When we were taught a song, we had to learn the meaning of each sentence. Even today, if six of us from my generation sing in the choir, it will sound like forty people. Another thing, we even sound good without music. When you know, why you are singing for the Lord, it makes a difference. For us, it does not take a huge number because we were taught to give our all to God. Our Youth Choir would sing at Mt. Pilgrim Baptist District and all across the city. We always had the support of our family and church family. It would not be one or two people supporting us, we went all over as a large, loving supportive family.

Another childhood memory is going to get chairs down to place down both sides of the aisle when Reverend Oden would preach. Grandmama and all of the ladies would be shouting. The Spirit would be high! I can't forget those times.

Even though I am an adult, I love Rushing Spring because it is a no judgement, free zone. We will love you despite whatever you have going on – we are a true family. Although Granddad is deceased, when I turn left onto Rushing Spring Road, I still get excited because I get to see my family and friends.

I feel that we at Rushing Spring have now made a full circle because we were in need of a little food for our soul and we got it. It is a blessing to get to see our childhood friend, Victor, who grew up in the church to serve as our seventh Pastor. I feel that he is a visionary and in my family, we feel that Pastor Lewis is a warhorse for the Lord! Pastor Lewis is not just preaching, but he is teaching. If you listen to him teach the Word, you cannot help, but to grow in the Lord. We leave church feeling reassured that God is able. I will tell anybody, who wants to hear the Word that they should stop by Rushing Spring Baptist Church to come see a man named Dr. Victor Lewis, who is loving, friendly and teaching God's Holy Word.

Jetter Brown

"Sister Jetter Brown loves God and has a pure heart. She is not a blood relative, but she loves Rushing Spring as we do. It is okay for her to be in the book." – Charles D. Avery, Sr.

I FIRST ATTENDED Rushing Spring Baptist Church in 1988 or 1989. I can vividly remember that when I entered the door, I felt love. I recall Sister Elgertha Byrd, Sister Vivian Booker and Sister Jerri Avery welcoming me. When they greeted me, I could feel they were being sincere and these women helped to encourage me to get involved with the church. Everyone I encountered was very friendly. When I first started attending, Sister Sue Embry was the Sunday School Superintendent and she was the one along with Brother Charles Avery, Jr., who encouraged me to get involved in the Sunday School Ministry.

I really enjoyed attending Sunday School, and Sister Embry saw a special gift within me. As a result, I soon became a Sunday School Teacher and Youth Advisor. I worked closely with Deacon Lesley Ford and together, we thought of ideas to enhance the Youth Ministry. Sister Donzetta Avery and Sister Maxine Brown played a major role in assisting us. The Deacon Ministry was very supportive of our new ideas. We felt the youth needed to have fun, while learning the Word of God.

As a unified team, we assigned church homework to the kids. The kids had such activities as learning the church covenant, church history, Ten Commandments and Bible verses. If the kids did not complete their church homework, they could not participate in fun, rewarding activities, such as bowling, skating, and fun outings.

It was important to us for the kids to learn the importance of being a servant for God. I can recall when the Isom family had a house fire. We had the kids to go over and help the family. The kids enjoyed serving others and they are still serving others. It is a blessing to know we placed a seed into the lives of these kids.

My fondest memory was going to Six Flags with the youth. The kids loved the roller coaster and so did Donzetta, but I was not getting on that rollercoaster. I truly enjoyed loading up my Honda Accord with the kids and thank God, we never received a traffic ticket! After Christmas practice, we took time with the kids to drive around and look at Christmas lights---there are so many fun memories.

One thing, I love about Rushing Spring is that when one hurts, everybody hurts. When my father died in 2004, I remember that practically, the entire church came to be with me during his funeral service. I will never ever forget that because when I turned around and could see my church family, it meant the world to me. I still pass on to my kids the love and knowledge, I received from Rushing Spring. I still consider Rushing Spring as my church home.

I cannot say it enough that Rushing Spring is a family of love. When I drive onto the premise, you are greeted with a smile and kindness. It is a privilege to have watched the current Pastor, Victor Lewis, grow up, right there at Rushing Spring. I want him to know that he is an encourager and I truly love him and Rushing Spring Baptist Church.

Stanley Peterson

"I love everyone on Brown Hill. On Sunday evenings, I would take my children for a walk to Brown Hill because I felt in my heart it was important for them to know their folks. If you do not know where Brown Hill is back off in the woods, you will never find it. Growing up, we loved being around Aunt Mamie, Aunt Nellie and Aunt Carrie; they were sweethearts.

Jesse Peterson, never married and raised most of his siblings' children. J. T. and I use to say, "Jesse go and get you a wife!" Jesse would just say, "I got to take care of Mama and these children. I'll keep a friend, but that's it."

When Charles Jr. pulls up in front of the church with me, I will hear Stanley's voice saying, "I am here to help you. I got you." Don't y'all let any man ever break the bond between a Peterson, Brown, Miller and Avery – we are family and have survived together." – Charles D. Avery, Sr.

FORGIVE ME, BUT IT IS HARD FOR ME to talk about Brown Hill and Rushing Spring without crying because I miss all of those old folks that are no longer here with us. I am the nephew of Jesse Peterson, really I was just like his son. Jesse Peterson, a black man, raised by himself, his nieces and nephews. He raised us in the home where he was born. The home would almost remind you of a shack with a front porch. I lived in our home with Uncle Jesse until he died on February 19, 2012. Uncle Jesse was a man of few words and he only dealt with family and a few members from Rushing Spring. He was also a World War II veteran. Jesse had such a strong impact on me and he encouraged me to enter the military.

Uncle Jesse Peterson's parents were Mark Sr. and Mamie Brown Peterson, who lived on Brown Hill. Mark Sr.'s parents were Shack Peterson and Martha Ann Powell. Mamie's parents were Belle Brown and Dean Brown, whose first names, some say in the late 1800s and early 1900s were Eugene and Betty Jean.

Mamie's sisters and brothers were Percy, Jean, Daniel "Dan", and Rosa Lee. Carrie was their cousin, but she grew up in the same house with them and they called Aunt Carrie their sister. All of Mark's and Mamie folks attended Rushing Spring Baptist Church. My family started attending Rushing Spring from the very beginning. Mark Peterson's family is related to the Goins family, who owned Rushing Spring.

Uncle Jesse's siblings were Mark Jr., Alice, David, Andrew, Jenny, Eunice, Doris and Betty Jean. Few people know that Brown Hill was a prosperous black community back in the day. Mark Sr. worked for the Alabama By-Products and on our land they sold vegetables and animals. All of the Peterson's, including the girls, worked hard. Uncle Jesse's sisters were very pretty to me.

My mother, Doris Peterson Payne knew Uncle Jesse would provide the family with whatever we needed. My mother had eight children, Cassandra, Alice Denise "Nita", then me, Veronica, Kevin, Sharon, Randy and Scheleta. My dad, Gene Brown was older and not around to raise me. My dad was from a different set of Brown's from North Birmingham and he relocated to Ohio. I never missed out on having a father around because of my Uncle Jesse.

In his younger days, Uncle Jesse prepared our meals and made cornbread from scratch that would melt in your mouth. Uncle Jesse had a way of mixing that cornbread with tons of butter. Sometimes as a joke, church members would say to him, "Hey, Cornbread, how are doing?" Uncle Jesse would just laugh and his cigar never fell out of his mouth.

His collard greens were the best. He said, "If you want your collard greens to be tender, it is all in the way you cut the greens, Cut them real fine and watch how they turn out." He also cooked poke salad made from pokeweeds. The pokeweeds grew by the train track and we would have fun going to find it. Pokeweeds are poisonous, but Uncle Jesse knew how to prepare it and that was a treat for us.

Jesse lived a simple life up until he died. Some may have thought we were poor, but Brown Hill taught us how to survive and trust God. Our Uncle Jesse ain't never been broke and he worked hard for his money. It was nothing for our Uncle Jesse to work a double shift. If you asked Uncle Jesse for something, he would always pull out a roll of hundreds, straight from his pocket. Jesse made sure we had our necessities. He would give you whatever you needed. I saw Uncle Jesse help the church and some of the members financially, but he did not ever brag or gossip about it.

When you saw Jesse, he was driving a pick-up truck, had his hat on and was either headed to Food Giant in Tarrant City, work, church or home. A few times, he would go downtown and listen to music. He never missed attending the annual City Stages Music Festival and would go by himself. He loved running into our church family when he would attend. Any of them, will tell you Uncle Jesse enjoyed his life.

Uncle Jesse's rule to his nieces and nephews was to go to school, go to work and go to church. When Uncle Jesse came thru the doors at Rushing Spring, all of his nieces and nephews were right there with him. We were not raised to go to church and just sit down. Uncle Jesse said, "Find something to do at church." Right now, my sister Veronica and cousin, Vernessa and I are ushers at Rushing Spring Baptist. I also help park cars when we have big events. Whenever, I am not working on my job, you will find me at Bible Study on Wednesday nights. We know the Word at Rushing Spring, Pastor Lewis does not sugar coat it.

UNCLE SYLVESTER "BUSTER" BROWN started back attending Rushing Spring in 1957 when he relocated his family from Montgomery, AL. Uncle Sylvester married Prentella Brown, who was our Sunday School Teacher. Aunt Prentella passed all, I mean all of her biblical knowledge to her daughter, Maxine Brown.

Uncle Sylvester use to work for the cement plant in L&N City near Tarrant. Uncle Sylvester, Aunt Prentella and Cousin Maxine lived in walking distance to the cement plant. Bernice Miller Young, his niece lived next door. Eventually, the cement plant purchased all the homes near the cement plant and Uncle Sylvester was able to move again into a home next door to his mother, Nelly Woods Brown. Aunt Nelly was the sister to Shelly Woods Avery. Aunt Nelly's parents were Marian and Kizzie Woods. Cousin Charles Sr. taught us that Mama Shelly told them that Marian and Kizzie Woods were from plantations near Roebuck and Woodlawn.

Aunt Nelly lived on Brown Hill when she was married to Uncle Sylvester's father, Curtis "Will" Brown., Sr. I do not know the year Uncle Curtis Sr. died. However, Aunt Nelly later married Square Wise and relocated to L&N City. Everyone talked about how they missed Aunt Nelly living on Brown Hill because she was known for quilting, crocheting and cooking. She cooked for anyone that stopped by. Before working for the cement plant, Uncle Sylvester was a Mess Sergeant in World War II, which meant he was in charge of the kitchen. He was able to use the recipes passed down from his mother while cooking for soldiers. Aunt Nelly was living when her son, Uncle Sylvester died in 1965. Aunt Nelly died in 1970.

Aunt Nelly's daughter, Gaston lived on Huntsville Road, which was one or two streets over from Aunt Nelly's home. Gaston married Nathan Young. After marrying, they moved to Leeds, AL.

Aunt Nelly and Uncle Curtis Sr. had other children. Their daughters Rosetta and Eda Mae and son, Curtis Jr. lived in Collegeville. Everyone called Curtis Jr. by the nickname of "Simp". Simp spoke with a whisper due to a military injury. We may have called Rosetta, "Tootsie". The daughter, Margaret did not have children and lived in North Birmingham, not far from 32nd Street North. Rosetta's children still come over to Rushing Spring for special days. I keep in contact with Rosetta's side and Charles Jr. still hears from Rosetta's daughter.

My generation can vividly remember Aunt Nelly's daughter, Dosia Brown Miller because she attended Rushing Spring with her family. When Aunt Dosia walked in, she sometimes sat on the middle pew to the left of the church. Cousin Dosia was a sharp dresser and would sit to the left of the church.

Cousin Dosia's husband was Fate Miller. Fate Miller and Percy Brown worked at the Ketona Rock Quarry with Aaron Brewster. I think he was there when Aaron Brewster died on the job. Aunt Dosia's children were

Bernice Miller Young and Otis Miller, Sr.

NO ONE FROM RUSHING SPRING will ever forget the brothers, Fate and Julius Brown, who were the sons of Aunt Carrie. These brothers are my cousins and they lived next door to Uncle Jesse. Fate always took the lead of Julius Brown. Julius Brown was a ladies man, who was a large in size and tall in height. He had a way of talking to you always with a smile. When we use to walk in church, we always saw Cousin Fate sitting quietly to the right, near the window. Julius did most of the talking for Fate. Their parents were George and Carrie Brown. Fate and Julius had other siblings, but these two made their mark at Rushing Spring. When Uncle Jesse sat in church, he always sat towards the back to the right near Cousin Fate.

Chapter 6

Solid Foundation

"I love all my nieces and nephews, but my older nieces must also help keep the family together by watching their tongue because the others will feed off what they throw out. They must help fix problems within the family by doing what is right. Now, my niece and nephew, Sue and Snook grew up in the house with me and my siblings so I want you to put Sue's daughters in the book. Let all of them know Uncle Charles loves them." – Charles D. Avery, Sr.

Janice & Cheryl

MY SISTER, JANICE AND I along with our brother, Napoleon Jr. "Junebug or Nap" grew up being guided by our parents, grandparents and great-grandparents. Our great-grandparents lived down the hill from Rushing Spring Baptist Church and this is where we have always worshipped. Mama was a member of Rushing Spring Baptist and Daddy was a member of Ebenezer Baptist Church located in Ketona. We grew up living in the Airport neighborhood and when our Mama drove us to visit our great-grandparents, which was practically every day, we got excited when we the car jumped over the train tracks in Ketona and then turned left onto Rushing Spring Road, even Mama got excited.

Our great grandmother, Mama Shelly was a divine, inspirational, virtuous woman, who taught us what was right. As a small child, I can remember Mama Shelly and the older women of the church placing their hands on me and praying that I would receive the Holy Ghost. Let me tell you, I felt it as a child and I still got the Holy Spirit within me. Back then, women led by example and they meant business. Janice remembers when I was baptized at the age of five, right there at Rushing Spring on top of the hill.

Janice and I both remember when our brother took ill as a child. Papa went to the altar and got on his knees to pray for Nap's healing. After church, we went to the hospital to visit Nap and the doctor said that he started feeling better around 11:00 a.m. That was the same time, Papa was praying.

Cheryl, Junebug, and I grew up under Rev. Fitzhugh J. Herron. Rev. Herron was our Pastor and was known for walking to church. He often wore a black suit, white shirt, black boots, and black hat. Cheryl and I still remember him saying, "A hypocrite is like a straight pen, he is headed one way and pointed another way." Once a year, he preached a sermon entitled, "The High Cost of Low Living." He often said, "Train your children so more than you will love them." Oh, and he said, "Even a bird has sense to build a nest before having children." Rev. Herron taught us the facts of life.

You have never heard anyone say anything negative about Rev. Herron. Rev. Herron put forth an effort to spend quality time with every family within the church. Janice, really Rev. Herron was like a grandfather to everybody, he was funny, even-tempered and tried to help us by teaching us the Word. Our beloved, Rev. Herron died in 1971.

Cheryl and I learned some infamous sayings from Mama Shelly that we still live by. If you were hurting Mama Shelly would say, "That's alright, we are not going to worry about it" and another saying was, "If you do right, right will follow you." She often said, "If you will steal, you will kill, if you lie, you will do just about anything." Another saying, she had that remains in my heart, "Do not intentionally hurt anyone because sometimes their feelings are all they have." Mama Shelly did not have a lot of education, but she was wise. I was even able to use her wisdom when teaching my students in the classroom and even when I am talking to people on the phone. People in the church still talk about Mama Shelly and she died around 1976, but her legacy is still alive. You cannot say anything negative about Mama Shelly. All you can say is she loved her family and Rushing Spring Baptist Church.

Janice, you left out that Mama Shelly was known for growing beautiful flowers. She treated her flowers with love and respect. Mama Shelly would place fresh floral arrangements on top of the organ and piano at the church.

Janice and I remember how Mama Shelly & Papa's house would be packed on Sunday's after church with all of the Avery's and our church family. Everyone had to go pass, Tip, the dog to get into the house. Later, Mama Shelly and Papa had a German Shepherd named Mickie, given to them by Uncle Rec.

I vividly remember on most Sundays, our family friends, Sister Sarah King, Brother Leonard King, Sr. and their children, Peggy and Leonard Jr. would stop by after church. We called Leonard Jr. by the name of Bubba. The King family would come in and out of the house, just like they were an Avery. Even though, they were not blood relatives, we loved them as though they were. We forgot about them being a King.

Down at Mama Shelly and Papa's house, everyone would either sit on the front porch, living room, dining room or kitchen. For those, who did not come inside the house, they would stop in the front yard to say a few words to everyone. Everyone, who entered the house was offered a glass of lemonade or water. Mama Shelly taught us how to be hospitable to our guests. We were all guaranteed a home cooked meal too from Mama Shelly. Mama Shelly could cook! Janice, remember how Mama Shelly would make the best meatballs for our soup. She always served a side of cornbread with her soup. Cheryl, do not forget the hamburger patties with rice and gravy. Another thing, Janice, remember the homemade biscuits with butter. Cheryl, one more thing, remember the homemade pound cake that would melt in your mouth. Wait Janice, this is the last one, remember Mama Shelly's apple cobbler!

Mama Shelly was big on canning food. Janice and I watched Mama Shelly can corn, peas, tomatoes, apples, peaches, grapes, and blackberries. She always made a special homemade jelly. Cheryl, you remember how Mama Shelly's sisters would talk real proper and say, "Oh Shelly, wow, did you make this jelly?" We would fall out laughing at them.

DURING THE HOLIDAYS, all of Mama Shelly's sisters would be in town and the house would be packed and everyone from Ketona and Rushing Spring would come to visit. Janice, Nap, and I were right there too, along with our cousins, Singleton "Junior" and Ronnie. On Sunday, during the holiday season, we almost had to push our way to get inside the house because there were so many people.

When we entered Mama Shelly's front door, we could smell apples ripening, fresh flowers and food baking in the oven. I cannot let go of those days in my mind. We truly loved our cousin, Perry, who really acted like a big brother. Perry was always in charge of cutting down our Christmas tree. Perry would go on the hill to chop down the Christmas tree and we would start cheering! Cheryl would say, "Perry, chop that tree!" Once he picked up that tree, we would run behind Perry holding our Christmas tree.

CHERYL WAS FORTUNATE because Mama Shelly kept her before she started school. Mama Shelly's sister, Aunt Lozzie Woods Brown lived by the church, next door to Cousin Nettie. Aunt Lozzie did not have kids and considered Cheryl as her baby. Aunt Lozzie was known for being tough! She always dipped tobacco. One time, Cheryl got hold of her tobacco and got sick. We had to put Cheryl to bed because she had a bad stomach ache from Aunt Lozzie's tobacco.

Janice and I always say that Aunt Lozzie probably was the first person that ever cursed aloud during Sunday service. Someone made a mistake and stepped on her big toe. Aunt Lozzie said that curse word with the big letter, *S*. She said, "S***, someone stepped on my big toe!" Everybody turned their head because Aunt Lozzie cursed in church, but all of us knew Aunt Lozzie had bad feet with corns on her toes. During the week, Aunt Lozzie wore shoes with her toes out, but on Sunday, since she was the head usher, she wore black, leather pumps.

I am the only niece that can mimic Aunt Lozzie walking because her hips were huge and when she entered the church, she knew all eyes were on her. Janice, wouldn't Aunt Lozzie strut and her hips would just roll baby! As she walked, her head would turn side-to-side as she smiled at you.

In the end, she fell ill from a stroke. She had the stroke while bringing in coal and wood into her home. The stroke affected her memory and they thought she would come around if she set her eyes on me. Mama took me to the hospital and I got on the bed with her. I said, "Aunt Lozzie, it is Cheryl. It is me, Aunt Lozzie! Cheryl!" I remember being so hurt that she did not recognize me and soon she died.

Cheryl, we must mention Aunt Honey. Aunt Honey was another sister of Mama Shelly and she was a rough rider. That woman had no fear! Don't let somebody make Aunt Honey and Aunt Lozzie mad because together or separately they would be ready for war. Aunt Honey would bring our cousin, Pam with her whenever she visited. Pam looked like a beauty queen.

I feel privileged because we got to enjoy several of Mama Shelly's sisters. Let's see, we met Aunt Ida, Aunt Mary, Aunt Nellie, Aunt Honey, Aunt Lonnie and Aunt Lozzie. All of them taught us class, style, dignity, and self-respect. While I am talking this just hit me, I would like for somebody in the family to find out whatever happened to Ned and Ted, Aunt Lonnie's grandkids from Bessemer, AL because they spent a lot of time with us in Rushing Spring and we stopped hearing from them after she died.

Janice and I will be forever grateful to those souls, who are gone on to glory. Every day, I think of them, especially my grandmother, Odell. My grandmother lived in North Chicago and she visited Rushing Spring every summer. When she arrived, she came to Mama Shelly's to work. My grandmother would paint, put down new linoleum flooring, hang new curtains and place new bedspreads on the beds. My grandmother was a giver and believed in sharing.

I often tell Cheryl that I am thankful that our parents, Napoleon and Sue Embry allowed a village to help raise us. That entire village, including the church, made us, who we are today. My brother became an engineer, I retired as a school teacher and Cheryl retired as a social worker. We were raised to become servants to God's children. We all need to use our God given gifts to help somebody.

Uncle Charles was in our village. Whenever we went to talk to Uncle Charles, he would say, "Sit right here baby." He prayed for all of us and today, Janice and I pray daily for the family. I can remember Uncle Charles walking to church with all of his kids, not just one Sunday, but every Sunday.

As I grow older, I tell Janice that I want the family to remember our dedication to Rushing Spring and we tried to treat people right. My sister and I want others to remember us like they remember our mother because Mama will always be known for having a direct line to Jerusalem!

WHEN I AM LONG GONE, my words are to my younger cousins, Lamar, A.J. and Jewaun. To the three of you, remember your Cousin Cheryl sincerely loves you and as you mature, I want you to become Avery men that are known for helping to take care of Rushing Spring. Please remember the words of Mama Shelly, "Do right, so right will follow you." Then, think of Anthony Avery, Sr. when raising your family. Anthony set an example of how you should provide for your family in life and in death. You three witnessed firsthand, how Anthony loved his family and Rushing Spring.

Continue to teach your children about Jesus and teach them the family history. When the three of you decide to marry someone, turn to the Bible and read how a virtuous woman should live and then read about the Fruit of the Holy Spirit. Together, with your future wives, pull out the Bible because it will tell you anything you need to know. Your blood and souls are drenched in the Holy Spirit, don't fight it – just use it in your daily walk.

Junior and Vickie

"I want Junior in the book because he is the son of my oldest sister, Sena Avery Lewis. All of us called her Auntie and even her son calls her Auntie. Junior and Vickie raised their children in Rushing Spring. Their son, Victor got the Holy Ghost over in Rushing Spring and one day he will return." – Charles D. Avery, Sr.

I HAVE ALWAYS ENJOYED MUSIC and I started playing for Rushing Spring when I was thirteen years old. I started off playing two Sundays each month. Rev. Herron preached the first and third Sunday of each month at Rushing Spring. When Rev. Herron was not at Rushing Spring, he was preaching at Shiloh Baptist Church in West End. My wife, Vickie grew up attending Shiloh and her childhood home is right by the church. I always thought it was ironic that we both grew up under the same Pastor and we lived in different directions.

Junior started bringing me to Rushing Spring to visit in the late 1960s. I could not believe people were still using outdoor toilets. I was a city girl and everyone, who visited Papa and Mama Shelly had to go in the backyard to use the outdoor toilet. Even behind the church were two outdoor toilets, one for the ladies and one for the men.

It felt like I was going back to the olden days. It was unreal! Junior grew up in Rushing Spring, but it took me some time to get adjusted to it. Years past and I can remember when Snoot came to Papa's home and tore down his outdoor toilet and plumbing was then installed at Papa's home. The indoor bathroom was then located behind the back bedroom.

Vickie, you are talking about the outdoor toilets, but what about the pigs near the outdoor toilets behind the church. Before Uncle Verbin built his home behind the church, the Avery's kept pigs over there in a fence. When you went in the back of the church to use the toilet, you could smell the pigs and see them waddling in the mud.

My Uncle Shep's home was near Papa's home. You could always see Uncle Shep working in the vegetable garden. He always kept corn and did not mind sharing. Uncle Rec would grow his vegetables near Uncle Shep's garden. Uncle Rec enjoyed growing collards greens, mustard greens, watermelons, cantaloupes, tomatoes, and squash. Uncle Rec would say, "When you cook greens, put just a little bit of sugar in the pot to give them a good taste."

Before Mama Shelly died, she would even grow her greens down the walkway located near her front porch. All of them taught us that our garden needs to be located in an open area where there is plenty of sunshine. You never plant crops in a shaded area.

Junior convinced me to move into an empty home at Rushing Spring in 1982. Together, we raised our family in Rushing Spring. We have six children, Simona, Singleton III, Norma, Victor, DeWayne, and Victoria. I went in labor with DeWayne and Victoria while living in Rushing Spring.

Most of the older people in Rushing Spring were dead and we did not have many neighbors. The only neighbors we had were Auntie, Papa, Verbin's family, Cousin Nettie Lee and William Lee. Uncle Levi's house was still standing and it reminded you of a shotgun house.

My mother, Auntie moved back home to be with Papa after Mama

Shelly died. Papa was so hurt when Mama Shelly died in 1976. After she died, Papa did not talk as much. To me, he was more talkative when she was around.

When I told Junior, I would live in Rushing Spring, I had no idea I would wake up to the sounds of roosters crowing at daylight. I was not prepared for the number of lizards that lived in those woods. When I washed clothes and hung them up, I would have to shake the lizards off the clothes. Again, here I am a city girl dealing with lizards so my solution was I was no longer hanging our clothes outside.

Vickie, I remember you were outdone that we had to use the well pumps for our drinking water and bathwater. Back then, Uncle Verbin's well pump would push our water up and our well pump would push the water down; the two pumps worked together. I taught all of my kids how to pull out a well pump, which was about 100 feet deep. The kids and I had to work together to pull out the well pump, which was work and they did not mind helping. All of them should remember having to prime the well pump with water once we pulled it out. All of us would be exhausted after working with those well pumps.

While Junior was at work, I had to learn how to start a fire to keep us warm. Snoot showed me the proper way to start the fire. Snoot would also come and cut our wood for us. One year, we got snowed in and I prayed we would not run out of wood because I did not want to help Junior cut down more wood. Look at me, I am a pretty woman and was a former majorette and I did not want to cut down wood! My siblings were amazed at how we were living.

I will say that I am thankful that I never had to worry about someone bothering our children, especially when Junior was away working. Our children were always safe in Rushing Spring. I did not even have to peep out of the window to check on them. It was a joy to see, Victor, DeWayne and their cousin, Jewaun riding on one bike up and down the hill at Rushing Spring. They were free to run and play all over Rushing Spring.

Since we lived near the church, our children were very active in the church. I was active with the singing in the choir while Junior played the organ. I enjoyed singing on our Annual Women's Day. It was a joy to me to be able to direct the Children's Choir. The children loved to sing, "Don't let the Devil Ride." We had one of the best Children's Choirs in Tarrant City.

WHEN I BECAME PREGNANT WITH VICTOR, I did not know I was pregnant. Junior and I were standing together at Clarks Temple. Bishop Cunningham's wife walked over to me and told me I was pregnant. She told me that my child was anointed by God and he does not belong to you – that's God's child. When the doctor confirmed I was pregnant, guess how many months I was? Six months!

I went into labor with Victor on a Friday and I only had one pain in my lower back. Victor was born on Junior's lunchbreak at Brookwood Hospital. Sister Bonner that now attends Rushing Spring was a nurse at the hospital during his delivery.

Victor has always been different. Even at the age of five years old, Victor would continuously read his Bible. By the time he was seven or eight years old, he would be in bed with a flashlight reading his Bible.

Victor has never given me any trouble, I mean absolutely no problems.

He has never raised his voice to any of us. Since he was a child, he cannot stand conflict and argument. He will remove himself from the situation. He often says, "I serve a God of peace and you must shake off the dust from your feet."

Victor always spent time with older, seasoned preachers. Uncle Rector was very influential in accepting Victor's gift while he was still a young boy. Victor loves learning and wants to pour his knowledge into his members. Again, I am just thankful that God chose Vickie Lewis as his mother. I am forever thankful.

WHEN I DIE, I want all of the children I gave birth to and my grandchildren to look at all of our mistakes and try not to make the same mistakes. I want all of them to have a good, clean life. When a mother looks at her children and they are doing well, it makes her heart feel good, but when your children ain't doing well in life that ain't no good feeling. Each generation should do better than the previous generation. I demand all of mine to continue being devoted to working for the Lord and please do what is right because God is watching.

I must end by saying that I am thankful that God chose me to give birth to Dr. Victor Sinclair Lewis, Sr., the seventh Pastor of Rushing Spring Baptist Church. Who would have thought that my child would reach masses of people because of his anointing sent by God? I am honored that I am his mother.

Chapter 7

Lucille's Kids

"Lucille Avery's children and grandchildren really need to be in the book. Let me think, you might want to get at least two children and two grandchildren, call those that you know and they will talk to you. You see, Lucille was married to my second cousin, Wesley Avery and she is the first cousin to Mama Shelly. Lucille and Mama Shelly's maiden name was Woods. Now, Wesley Avery was named after his daddy, who was my Uncle Lee.

I always admired the fact that even after Wesley's death, Lucille kept her family together --- she was the glue. Think about this, Lucille is long gone, been gone on, but she is still ruling her family from the grave. Her children know they better do what is right. All of them have done well and it makes me feel good to know their roots are from Long Street, right here in Ketona. To me, Lucille is a good example for any single woman raising her family the right way."

– Charles D. Avery, Sr.

Bertha Lula & Brenda Faye

BRENDA WILL TELL YOU that whenever I think of Ketona, I think of *home-home-home*! You know when you are home, you should always feel love, peace, and togetherness. As far as I am concerned, Ketona has always represented the meaning of home. Regardless of how poor some of us were, everyone stood together. None of us felt that we were poor because whatever we did not have, you already knew that a neighbor would help. Ketona from our era was always a tight-knit community. No one in Ketona kept to themselves because we are all one, family unit.

Bert, do you remember how we would step on anyone's front porch and the lady of the house would holler thru the door or window, "Come on in." I mean all the ladies said it the same way, it was like a song, "Come on in." There were a lot of times when we would walk by a neighbor's home and join them to sit on the porch. We gained wisdom from our older neighbors because we could ask questions and we always received an acceptable answer. No one was allowed to walk past a home and not speak. Greeting our neighbors was mandatory. We received this kindness from every household.

Think about it, Ketona is only two streets and one road. Back then, the black community of Ketona could live on Pine Hill Road, Long Street, and Rose Street. All of our homes were so close together and someone was always watching you. Everyone was safe in Ketona; we knew no one would bother us. No one locked their doors because we were safe, whether it was during the daytime or nighttime. Stop for a moment and just think about the weaving of a quilt, we were so close knit that we were all part of the woven fabric. Everyone had a sense of camaraderie and closeness. Although my sisters live out-of-state, Bert, Jean, and I are over seventy years of age, but we still reminisce weekly over the phone about our Ketona. I am excited right now talking about Ketona. I miss our Ketona!

We were blessed that we had so many strong, black men that looked after each other, in addition to their very own household. The majority of black men that lived in Ketona and Rushing Spring went to church with their family and were active in their children's school activities. Brenda, do you remember how Daddy made learning fun? Yes, Bert, I remember Jean and I would get under the dining table and eagerly await Daddy to roll oranges to us. Daddy had a way of teaching us how to count by having us count the seeds in our orange. Bert, Daddy also had excellent penmanship when printing and even today, I print just like Daddy. Daddy took pride in writing and could write just like a calligrapher. Another thing, Daddy only had an eighth grade education, but even when he got off from work, Daddy along with Mother took the time to sit down at the dining room table to teach us. I remember Daddy after work, taking time to teach all of us our State capitals while sitting at the dining table. Yes, Bert he did and in our household learning was fun and was not considered a chore.

Daddy worked for L&N Railroad that came thru Ketona and that was not an easy job, but he always came home ready and eager to spend time with his family. Brenda, another good thing about Daddy working for the railroad was that we all received free passes to ride the train and he earned enough money to purchase the first car in Ketona.

ONE SPECIAL PERSON that stands out is Mrs. Beulah Allison and everyone from Ketona affectionately called her, "Granny". Granny was born around 1893 and died in 1985. Bert, wouldn't you agree that Granny was a granny to everyone, regardless of your age? Yes, Brenda, she was a midwife, a nurse, a helper, and a friend. Granny was a close friend to Mama Julia Davis. Brenda, what was Granny's husband name? His name was Thomas Allison and Cousin Charles named his oldest son, Tom after Granny's husband.

Our household attended Ebenezer Baptist Church and we all love to watch Granny bake the unleavened bread for Communion. Communion was held every first Sunday and we knew exactly when Granny would be baking the unleavened bread. Bert, I still know how to prepare the unleavened bread just like Granny.

When making the unleavened bread, Granny would mix plain flour, just a little oil and not too much water in a large bowl. She would then roll this mixture into a big ball of dough and then roll out the dough. When explaining why we used unleavened bread, Granny would say, "Brenda, Jesus was not puffed up and he was an ordinary, humble man." Granny would place this bread into a basket and once she got to church, she would place the bread onto a plate with a white cloth. The Pastor and Deacons would wash their hands and then break the bread in order to serve the members. The kids always looked for the largest piece to eat during Communion.

Granny was considered the Mother of Ebenezer Baptist Church and whatever Granny's hands touched, she did everything with love. When many of us were born, Granny's hands were the first to touch our bodies because she was Ketona's midwife. Granny was so humble and when she became ill everyone in Ketona cared for her until the very end. Granny's life was an example that we can all live by the Fruit of the Holy Spirit—it is not hard to do. Ketona's Granny made it into heaven because we know she is still our earthly Angel. No one should ever, ever forget Granny.

Ebenezer Baptist Church is home for us. It is so near and dear to our hearts because of the precious memories and we still get to see those we love. When it was time for me to join Ebenezer Baptist Church, Sis. Ada Jemison was sent to speak with me. Sis. Jemison was known in Ketona for walking and carrying a basket on her head. I can see her now sitting with me saying, "Bertha Lula, are you sure? Don't you play with the Lord!" I replied by saying, "I will not play with the Lord."

ANOTHER MEMORY for me Brenda is Cousin Odell. I do not know if you remember, but Cousin Odell and Mose Whitson lived next door to us. Our childhood home was once a double tenant home. It just hit me that Mose Whitson's dad was a preacher that lived on Pine Hill Road. As a girl, I spent a lot of time with Cousin Odell. One afternoon, Cousin Odell was in charge of keeping me and was supposed to feed me too. We sat at the table talking and having so much fun, that she did not have time to feed me before I left to return home. Guess what she did? She took some fatback and rubbed it across my mouth so it appeared that I had something to eat. I was so hungry during the night, but I played like everything was okay because I was ready to go back with Cousin Odell to chat.

I can also remember when Cousin Odell cleaned Mose's shoes and put them in the oven to dry. She totally forgot about Mose's shoes and when she thought about it, the shoes were smoking. Cousin Odell ran to our home so upset saying, "Y'all, I forgot his shoes were drying in the oven; I was busy scrubbing my floors." Cousin Odell was frantic because Mose would be coming home soon. Once he arrived home, I am sure they argued, but back then they kept children out of grown folks' business. One thing is for sure and everyone knew Cousin Odell could take of herself. She was not going to take too much off anyone and soon Mose was gone.

After Cousin Odell moved, Cousin Verbin and his wife, Lois moved in with their kids, Vivian, Shirley, and Verbin Jr. Lois remained at the house with the kids, while Cousin Verbin attended Alabama State University. While he was attending college, his daughter, Vivian died as a young girl. He soon came back and all of them along with Cousin Odell relocated to North Chicago.

I AM OLDER THAN BRENDA so I can tell you just a little about my memories of our grandfather, Wesley "Lee" Avery, who you know as Uncle Lee and we called him Paw-Paw. Paw-Paw loved his family, but was very firm and stern. Even though, he was a strict disciplinarian, his children, and grandchildren were always surrounding him. Paw-Paw was a leader, active in his church and always working. Paw-Paw was very active with the Parent-Teacher Association at the school. When I knew him, he was almost disabled because his body was just tired from working. I remember that when I was a girl, Paw-Paw worked for white families doing odd jobs. Paw-Paw worked until his body would not let him. After he died, Daddy used Paw-Paw's walking stick.

BERT, WE MUST SPEAK about Mrs. Bennie "Estelle" Glasgow. She on her own changed her name to Estelle because a teacher told her that Bennie was not a girl's name. When speaking of Ms. Estelle, you can't help, but smile because she was a dear friend to Mother. Ms. Estelle lived on Long Street across from Ms. Inez's home. She was married to Major Glasgow and their son was David Glasgow. David played the piano and the Glasgow's kept a piano in their dining room. The Glasgow's home was painted white and they had an all brick chimney. The train track was in the backyard of their home.

Ms. Estelle's brother was Will "Bud" Correthers and his wife was Gatheline. Almost everyone in Ketona called Gatheline Correthers, "Mommie" and everyone pronounced it as Mom-mie—we all put emphasis on mie! When we said, Mom-mie everyone would know, who you were speaking of. The Correthers lived on Pine Hill Road across from Aunt Mattie Pearl. The Correthers' daughters were Delores, Willie "Mae", and Elizabeth. The Correthers' daughters were known for their long, pretty hair and pretty dresses. The Glasgow's and Correthers were active at Ebenezer Baptist Church.

Everyone from our era in Ketona watched the love story unfold between Willie "Mae" Correthers and Carl Turnbow. Carl lived on Long Street and was the son of Buddy and Alice Turnbow. Brenda, I think you will agree with the fact that Carl and Mae have been in love since they were small children. They still love each other as though they are newlyweds.

I THINK EVERYONE IN KETONA AND RUSHING SPRING loves the Lord. Brenda, I can never forget Ms. Emma Walker. She was known for making big, thick biscuits. During breakfast, she always served thick, black coffee. Another thing, Ms. Walker had the best fried chicken. When preparing the chicken to cook, she only used salt, pepper, and flour. Her kitchen was so tiny, but we would be glad to sit in her kitchen.

In front of Ms. Emma's home was a big apple tree. It was decided that she needed to relocate because a portion of her lot was needed for the new location for Cedar Grove. Ms. Emma was so devastated about this decision and this impacted her mentally. Even though, she remained in Ketona, she never was right after that. Today, we would say she became clinically depressed over the situation, but back then we just knew she was devastated and always sad. First, Cedar Grove was near the railroad track and then it went to Long Street. Ms. Walker's lot was needed to move the church over a couple of yards. Even though, Ms. Emma was devastated, she still joined Ms. Corine on the front porch to listen to us have devotion during school.

Cedar Grove was a nice size church with a large congregation. In the very front of the church were steep steps. Inside, the church were wooden benches for the members to sit. The choir loft had three rows of wooden benches. The men would arrive early to place wood and coal inside the coal stoves for heat. Mr. Albert Devers was a Deacon there. Mr. Chrisell attended Cedar Grove with his sister, Jenny and her children.

Although, our family attended Ebenezer, we were always welcomed at Cedar Grove and Rushing Spring. Our parents allowed a village to raise us. Even after Daddy died, Mother still allowed our village to instill values into us. Brenda and the rest of my siblings will tell you, we will always be forever grateful for the values and morals that shaped, who we are today. Ketona will forever remain in our hearts.

Jason Lockhart

KETONA IS A HUGE MELTING POT because most of us are family and if you are not blood-related, you are still considered family. Ketona was our safe haven. We never had to worry about our safety because everyone was family that looked out for each other. There is really no place like Ketona. Everyone from Rushing Spring and Ketona belongs to the same family and the same village. My brothers and I spent just about every day in Ketona on Long Street at my grandmothers' home. My grandmother was Lucille Woods Avery. My parents are Charles Lockhart, Sr. and Brenda Avery Lockhart. I grew up with my oldest brother, Chuck and youngest brother, Jarrod.

Both of my parents were educators and they worked in Bibb County, Alabama. My parents had to drive over one hour to get to work each weekday. My childhood home is less than ten minutes away from my grandmother's home. Growing up, our daily routine consisted of waking up at 5:00 am and by 5:30 am, we were headed out the door to load up in our parents' car to go to my grandmother's home in Ketona. Once we arrived at Grandmother's home, we walked thru the front door and went directly to our beds. We slept for about one hour until it was time for breakfast. Each morning, my grandmother had toast or bacon ready for us to eat. By 6:45 a.m., we were out the door headed to school.

I started out at Springdale Elementary School and graduated from Tarrant High School. Many of our neighbors' grandkids from Ketona were our classmates. We even had classmates we knew from Rushing Spring Baptist Church. We did not have many worries when we got to school because we went to school with those we considered family.

Once school was dismissed, everyone went to their grandparents' homes. Once my brothers and I entered the house, we spent around thirty minutes eating and catching up with our grandmother. We were in a hurry because we had to meet the kids for our daily kickball game. We took our kickball game seriously. The kickball game consisted of us the Lockhart, Whatley, Turnbow, Relph, Holder, and Jones' families. Our elders even got excited about our kickball game. We played near Ebenezer Baptist Church. We always knew in our spirit when the kickball game was about to end and sure enough, Ms. Della's light blue car would soon pull up to pick up Puddin and Fred. Once they left our players were uneven and it was time to go back inside the house.

When we were not playing kickball, all of us spent time just walking up and down the street or going from house-to-house. Ms. Boot, Ms. LeeAnna, Auntie Mattie Pearl, Ms. Estelle, and others were influential in helping my parents and grandmother with our upbringing. Whenever we stepped on the front porch, someone always hollered, "Come on in." These women rarely left their homes, but knew everything that was going on. Our grandmother stayed on the phone most of the day with Ms. Estelle, her best friend.

I can remember that if anyone walked outside and did not speak to Ms. LeeAnna, everyone in the neighborhood knew you were in trouble. This is the thing, sometimes you did not know when Ms. LeeAnna would be sitting on her porch, especially when it was dusk dark because her porch was screened in and the porch would appear to be dark. However, if you caught a glimpse of her, you had better speak! I remember once I got caught walking across the train tracks when I should not have and Ms. LeeAnna caught me. I received the worse spanking from my grandmother, but again this is because our elders looked out for us. You did not have time to even try to think of doing anything mischievous. Mrs. Fleter Green known as Ms. Boot hardly ever went inside, but when I think about it now, she was looking out for us.

When I was coming up, I remember Mr. Pete and Ms. Jackie, who lived on Long Street across from my grandmother's home. Ms. Jackie was like a daughter to my grandmother. One thing that stands out is Mr. Pete kept a 12 gauge shotgun and loved to shoot squirrels. He would even wear raccoon hats. Mr. Pete and Ms. Jackie did not have indoor plumbing and their bathtub was located on their back porch, but they never went hungry and you never heard them complain. Everyone was welcomed into their home and they were not ashamed. Ms. Jackie praised the Lord every chance she could while serving at Ebenezer Baptist Church in Ketona. Whenever we saw them pull off in their 5 speed, green pickup truck, we knew they were headed to Tarrant City to shop. They were strong examples of how to survive and to not worry about keeping up with others.

IN THE YEAR, 2014, I had the opportunity to accept a lucrative job opportunity in Chicago, which meant I would have to relocate my wife and two daughters. The upbringing I received in Ketona helped me make the decision if we would relocate. Ketona helped mold me into the father that I am today and I grew up being surrounded by family. Growing up, I did not have a grandfather, but now my daughters have three grandfathers. I could not relocate my daughters away from their village. I want the elders that are now in my daughters' lives to have a strong impact on their upbringing.

As I grow older, I am thankful to God for my elders and Ebenezer Baptist Church located in Ketona for preparing me for life and fatherhood. Even though, Ebenezer Baptist Church and Rushing Spring Baptist Church are less than one mile apart, we grew up knowing each other and worshipping together. Most of us from Ketona are doing well and it is because of this village that taught us the love of God, self-worth, hard work and respect for our fellow man.

Jarrod Lockhart

I SPENT MORE TIME IN KETONA than my own childhood home. I will forever be grateful that God chose the Ketona community to serve as my strong foundation. To me, Ketona will always be a community of love and togetherness. Although Ketona is still in existence, the ways things were are long gone. None of us from Ketona had to worry about receiving negativity while playing in Ketona because we all protected each other. Nowadays, many of us do not see each other often because the majority of our grandparents are deceased, but we will always represent a strong, true village.

Our village consisted of men and women, who were our heroes, role models, disciplinarians, cheerleaders and molded all of us to become history makers. We were taught to be leaders and not followers. We were even taught to think outside the box and become innovators. Many of us are doing just that, we are making history by trying to help others and make a positive impact on society. Ketona in our eyes represented the definition of "true village". We had both men and women, who stressed the importance of education. We were all taught what is right and the importance of respecting and honoring our elders.

Grandmother always thought I could do no wrong. I was once pleasantly plump in size, but my grandmother influenced my self-love, self-worth, and self-esteem. Mrs. Lucille Avery was my motivator, encourager, and always showered me with love. In addition to my grandmother, Ms. Boot, Ms. Pearl Lee, Mr. Turk and really the entire Ebenezer Baptist Church impacted every aspect of my life. As a result, I am an educator that passes on the knowledge I received from Ketona to students I come in contact with. Ebenezer Baptist Church, my mother, and Ms. Pearl Lee had a major influence on my oratorical skills and even my memorization skills.

I must say something about Rushing Spring Baptist Church because it is an extension of my village. When the new edifice for Ebenezer Baptist Church was under construction, Rushing Spring Baptist Church opened its doors to us, in order that we could still worship together as a church family. They did this because in our village, we are taught to support each other and to be there for each other in our time of need. The teaching we received from across the train tracks in the heart of Ketona will live on forever.

Chapter 8

Ketona Students

Josephine Jones Scales

I STARTED TEACHING AT KETONA SCHOOL on my 21st birthday and this was my very first job. This job allowed me to purchase my first car, which was a Pontiac. I remained there teaching from 1956-1966 and truly loved my students. The first principal of Ketona School was Mercer A. Givhan, John McCain was the second principal, and the third principal was John S. Jackson. Mr. McCain only stayed around three years and pursued his PhD. Mr. Jackson left around 1966 or 1967 and was relocated to another school.

Our school served students from Ketona, Robinwood, Pinson, Airport, Brummitt Heights, Village Springs, and L&N City. L&N City stands for Louisville and Nashville Railroad and a lot of workers lived with their families in the L&N City Neighborhood. Students from the Airport started to attend during my first year of teaching. Ketona was different from all neighborhoods because just about everyone was related. If they were not related, you did not know it because this was a very close-knit community.

Students that still stand out to me because of their kindness and respectfulness are Charles Avery, Jr., and Faye Woods from Ketona. Another kind student was Carolyn Jones from L&N City. I remember teaching Carolyn's sister, Minnie during my first year of teaching at Ketona School. I also remember teaching the Booker children, who lived in Ketona on Pine Hill Road. Parents were heavily involved with their child's school. Mrs. Lucille Avery and Mrs. Margaret Woods were always at the school helping with anything we asked them to do. I attended college with Mrs. Avery's son, Wesley.

When I taught at Ketona School, girls could not wear pants. If we were going on a field trip, the girls could then change into their pants before boarding the bus for a field trip. Teachers always wore shoes with heels and stylish clothing. We did not wear dresses too far above the knee. Black teachers were always spotted shopping downtown at Blach's. Another department store, we all went to shop was Loveman's.

Ketona School had so many students and more black teachers were needed. Due to limited space, first and second grade classes were held at the area churches. Renovations at Ketona School started in 1956 and were completed in the spring of 1957.

We were excited to have a lunchroom added to our school in 1958. Prior to 1958, students brought their lunch to school. Once we got the lunchroom, we were provided good home cooking. Each Friday, we were served hot fish and butter beans. Soon after having the lunchroom, it had to go under county supervision. Once that occurred, the lunchroom staff had to follow regulated menus. The principal was in charge of selecting and hiring the lunchroom staff. Once the principal selected the lunchroom staff, they were approved by the Board of Education.

Our students behaved and enjoyed learning. My career there was spent teaching 7th grade Social Studies, 9th grade Alabama History and dance. My students were very smart and we won an award given by the State for our great work in Alabama history.

Dr. E. Paul Jones was in charge of all black teachers and his office was located on the 5th floor of the Masonic Temple near the Carver Theater. Black teachers had to go to his office to complete job applications for teaching positions. Dr. Jones had one secretary and was known for treating all black teachers like we were his own children. He took time to teach black teachers on what we could do and could not do. His wife was also a school teacher, who offered advice to incoming black teachers.

Back then, if you were a black woman, who worked as a nurse or teacher, you were well-respected. I feel that being a teacher is one of the most rewarding jobs on the planet, but you must be dedicated. It is important to show genuine concern for your students. Teachers must always study and be well-prepared to teach their materials.

Teachers must show self-respect, kindness and genuine support of each student. Regardless, of how involved parents are with the school, teachers must still motivate and encourage each student to do their very best work. When a student feels that a teacher genuinely cares, you will see a difference in the quality of work submitted by the student.

Carrie Jones Billups

I WAS REARED IN COLUMBUS, MS and graduated from Jackson State University. I taught in Mississippi for a total of twelve years. In 1960, I started teaching at Ketona School for a total of eight years. I taught sixth grade students. My daughter, Shelia started attending school there in the first grade and stopped attending in the fourth grade.

I remember how the homes in Ketona were so close together, they would catch on fire. It was amazing to see how the Ketona families always pulled together to help each other. These students excelled because the families were so heavily involved with their own kids and the kids of their neighbors. The parents of Ketona would come to the school and help the teachers decorate their classrooms prior to the new school year. We took a team approach in developing each student. You must have family and community support.

Teachers nurtured students and spent time with each student. We could paddle students and parents never complained. Some of the notable teachers while I was there were Mrs. Byrd, who attended Rushing Spring Baptist Church. Mrs. Horton taught third or fourth grade and Mrs. Reese taught third grade. Two male teachers that stood out were Mr. Anthony Henry and Mr. Arthur Baylor. Mrs. Stallworth and Mrs. Mullins taught sixth grade and Dr. McCain served as our principal. Most teachers had a Bachelor's degree and many of my colleagues went to Alabama A&M University to obtain their Master's degree.

Once I left Ketona School, I went to teach in Pinson, AL where I remained until retirement. I taught right at forty years. It is a joy to know that my knowledge was passed down to several generations of students.

Bertha Avery McKinney

AS STUDENTS, WE WERE TAUGHT to be excellent at all times. This was encouraged by our parents and neighbors. Our teachers taught us self-confidence, self-respect, and self-esteem. We took our school work seriously and teachers put the knowledge in our books into action. All of us will tell you, we enjoyed learning. Once, we enrolled at Hooper City High School, teachers would say, "That is a Ketona student." The students from Ketona understood we represented our community and family name.

My second grade teacher at Ketona School was Mrs. Lottie Love Vann Brewster from Village Springs, AL. We called her Mrs. Vann and she was known for nodding off to sleep during the morning hours because she was tired from her long commute. Mrs. Vann rode the school bus with Ms. Griffin to get back and forth from Village Springs. These ladies had to wake up early and then went to bed late. One fond memory, I have is Mrs. Vann Brewster had a real store in the classroom. She taught us how to count and make change.

Mrs. Burton taught sixth grade, ninth grade, and extracurricular activities. She taught us how to pour our hearts into writing. She took us on a field trip to Nashville, TN to meet and speak with the author, Arna Bontemps. Mr. Bontemps was well-educated and he gave us writing tips along with words to motivate us to do our very best. Mrs. Burton made history and writing come alive for us. She also took us to visit the home of Andrew Jackson. We were required to participate in oratorical competitions held in downtown Birmingham.

I was thrilled when Mrs. Burton chose me to interview her classmate,

Mr. Macon, who was a Tuskegee Airman. He amazed me with his words of wisdom and always used hand gestures when he spoke. I loved hearing about how his hands guided the airplane into battle. He went on to tell me how his airplane was shot down and as a result, he became disabled.

Donald Woods

"You need to find Doug Whatley or Donald Woods. I think at least one of them should be in the book. They are Ketona men, who are humble, work hard, and love the Lord." – Charles D. Avery, Sr.

THE KETONA SCHOOL, I REMEMBER had wooden buildings and a tin building with coal stoves. Mr. Ferguson from Robinwood was our janitor. His job duties included chopping wood and getting the coal ready for the stoves. My first job as a kid was to place the coal and wood inside buckets and take to each classroom.

Our largest building had four classrooms and a large auditorium with a large stage. The other building had classrooms too. Later down the years, one of the wooden buildings was bricked and still stands today. The brick building held the offices of the principal and secretary. We also took science courses in the brick building.

I started attending Ketona School in the first grade and left in the eighth grade. After leaving Ketona School, I attended New Castle High School and this school later changed its name to Springdale High School.

My family is originally from Oneonta, AL and I grew up on Long Street in Ketona. My parents were Edward Jr. and Margaret Woods. I grew up with my siblings, Ronald Edward, Benita and Helen Edwina. My father built our home on Long Street. In later years, when we moved to the Pine Knoll neighborhood in Tarrant, Dad built our new home. Dad also built additional homes in the Pine Knoll neighborhood for the Smiley, Mosley and Johnson families. My Dad along with other men from Ketona taught us to be hard working men! Even Rev. Herron from Rushing Spring took time to teach my sisters how to play the piano.

Regardless, of our age, we all remained obedient students, in and out of the classroom. We enjoyed learning wisdom from our elders on how to prepare to live our best life. We never got tired of learning and we always knew to never become disobedient.

My classmates and neighbors from Ketona are still my friends. My closest buddies growing up were Doug, Larry and Tony. We always had a good time! Now, when you saw Doug, you saw me! Our neighbor, Bobby Payne will always be known as the best deejay in Ketona because he kept us dancing in the street. We loved the Fourth of July holiday and at 12:00 pm, all kids from Ketona, came outside with their red, white and blue clothing. It was a joy to check out each other's outfits. We even had fireworks. Our teachers would even come back to the community to enjoy us on their vacation day from school.

As an adult, during one of my lowest points in life, Mr. Charles Avery, Sr. came to me and reminded me to remain humble and kind with my words. Even though, I was as adult, I was obedient and listened to wisdom. That is an example of how you never stop learning and growing. I can remember when his son, Charles Jr. gave me a job when I was in need of work. These two reminded me about humility because this is what we have been taught all of our life in Ketona and now we are passing down to our generations, what our elders taught us.

Chapter 9

Bro

"Bro must be in this book. He is my cousin, Mattie Pearl's oldest son and the grandson of Uncle Lee. I have always considered Bro as one of my sons because he grew up around me and I looked after him for his mama. Before Mattie Pearl died, she told me to look after Donnie. Tell all of Mattie Pearl's children, I love them and they got to have patience when caring for Donnie. Let Bro know I expect him to take care of his health because Rushing Spring and Little Vivian need him. I expect Bro, Charles Jr., and Tom to work together in harmony for the sake of the church." – Charles D. Avery, Sr.

MY NAME IS HENRY FORD BOOKER, JR. and everybody calls me "Bro", which is short for Brother. My entire life is centered on Ketona and Rushing Spring. I am the oldest son of Mattie Pearl Avery Shelton. I was in Mudear's belly when she married Henry Sr. and along came my sister, Patricia (Pat) and my brother, Harold. Those from Ketona and Rushing

Spring will tell you that when we were coming up everybody was in everybody's business, but you did not go around bad-mouthing each other because we were taught to protect each other. We were taught that rule from the time we could walk and talk. Even if you are not blood-related, which most of us are, we are not going to let anyone run over you. Many of us from my era are over the age of seventy, but we still protect and help each other.

There was no established Neighborhood Watch program in Ketona, but we all had our way of keeping up with each other by sitting on the front porch and walking the neighborhood. The mothers and grandmothers were housewives and knew everything that went on and they had no telephone. I always wondered how my grandmother, MaMa could find out what I was doing.

In Ketona, we did everything together. We even raised hogs and chickens together. I can remember my brother, Harold and I ringing the chicken's neck and then plucking the feathers off the chicken. We grew up living at my grandparents' home. We always had one cow, chickens, and hogs at our home.

Each morning, my job was to milk the cow. Our cow was named Susie. I remember we never let Susie go near green onions because you did not want smelly milk. I can remember having to churn milk to make butter and sweet milk. When I milked the cow, I made up musical beats like what you know as the hambone knee slap. I made up beats to help make it an easy workday.

When churning the milk, I had to use something like a broom handle with a wooden round piece. It reminded you almost of a plunger, but it did not have the rubber on it. Now listen at this, when the buttermilk turned yellow, the butter would float to the top and I would churn it just a little more to get it just right. When the cow wanted to stop producing milk for the day, you had to bring the calf to the cow because the cow always saved milk for the calf and you could get at least another gallon of milk.

I CAN REMEMBER MR. AND MRS. JOE EDDY, who lived in Ketona on Long Street. The Eddy's were always kind to the kids of Ketona. They always gave us homemade cookies, milk, and other treats. Mrs. Eddy was light brown, average height, weighed around one hundred and thirty pounds, and always wore an apron. Mr. Eddy was of average height and maybe around one hundred pounds. The Eddy's did not have children and they did not drive, but they lived very well.

The Eddy's always had eight or ten cows at one time. Cows were not cheap because most of us only had one cow at our home. Whites and blacks from all around Tarrant City bought milk and butter from them. Their home was the only two-story home in Ketona with four bedrooms and one bathroom.

It was in the 1950s when the Eddy's home caught fire and everyone, young and old cried. The fire started right before it was time for school to start. Tarrant City Fire Department came to help and even neighbors had their hose pipes spraying water, but we did not have the water pressure we needed to put out the fire.

Right now in my mind, I can see Mr. Fred Black hooking up the water hose to the spring trying to put out the fire. Mr. Fred Black was a white man and was the youngest of the Black brothers, who co-owned Ketona

Lumber Yard. Mr. Fred Black also owned the water rights to the spring located near Springdale Baptist Church.

The Eddy's ended up losing their home and lived with neighbors for a short period. The Eddy's continued working together and saved their money. This couple never missed a beat selling their milk and butter. Eventually, they had enough money to build a one-level home with two bedrooms and one bathroom. After their home burned down, I can remember Ed Woods, Jr. bricked his home because of the fire that happened at the Eddy's.

NEXT DOOR TO AUNT LUCILLE's house on Long Street was Ms. Corine and she was married to Allen White. Allen White was an example of a man that worked hard and walked wherever he had to go. When you saw him going to work, he always wore a work jacket. Look like, Mr. Allen might have worked for TCI, but double-check. Despite how hard he worked, the White family was very active at Ebenezer Baptist Church, which was near their home.

Will and Dave White were the brothers to Allen White. Dave White lived next door to Ellis "Doc Smitty" Smith on Pine Hill Road. The Whatley family lived next door to Dave White. Dave White did not have a wife and Granny fed him every day. Will White was known for cutting the men's hair and was married to Ms. Catherine. Will White's house was initially across the train track near the Spencer family. Later down the years, Will White moved next door to Ms. Mozette Grant on Rose Street.

Old Man Reese Davis lived next door to Coloreda's house in Ketona, which was across from the Correthers' home on Pine Hill Road. Old Man

Reese Davis married Ms. Julia, who was the mother of Theodore "Theo" Turk, Sr. Ladies of Ketona loved looking at Brother Theo Turk. He was so smooth and always wore nice suits. Brother Turk was known for singing "Peace in the Valley" at Ebenezer and Rushing Spring. Whenever he would sing, he put all of his heart into the song. It was in his blood to sing because his relatives were Sherman and Fred Hines. The Hines would go all over singing for the Lord. Brother Turk and family attended Ebenezer Baptist Church. He later joined Rushing Spring. Brother Turk's home is still standing on Rose Street.

Ms. Julia's sister was Mozette, who attended Rushing Spring. Ms. Mozette lived on Rose Street. Her daughter was Gladys Campbell, who served as an usher at Rushing Spring. Ms. Gladys married Charlie Campbell, who was not the nicest man in town, but we still treated him with respect. The Campbell's lived next door to Bill Battle, who was blind. Sam Wilform worked all of the time and lived next door to Bill Battle. Rose Street was very helpful in caring for Bill Battle.

Ms. Gladys married Charlie Campbell. The Campbell's lived next door to Ms. Mozette. A widow named Ms. Della Bella, who was known for making pecan pies for the neighbors lived near them. All of us loved Ms. Della Bella's pecan pies. Neighbors would even take their pecans to her house, in order that she had more than enough for the neighborhood pies. Ms. Della Bella would be so excited to prepare pies for all of us. She baked those pies with love.

Little Reese Davis was married to Ms. Luvenia "Chutter" and lived in a house with Old Man Reese Davis. Ms. Chutter was an usher at Rushing Spring. Ms. Chutter's sister was Ms. Rosie Lee, who was the mother of

Mildred. Ms. Rosie Lee took care of three generations of her family. Mildred's daughter was Mitzi Rae. Mitzi Rae is the mother to Candice, Bobby, and Erica, who attended Rushing Spring.

Old Man Reese knew the Bible. He could quote scriptures and taught us different stories in the Bible. He would sit outside on a large rock and teach us a lot of wisdom and we loved listening to him. All of us felt comfortable talking to him about anything. Now, we all witnessed when he would get a shot of liquor, Old Man Reese would put his finger in the air and get down dancing. Even though, he was having fun, he was right at home and not harming anyone.

AFTER SAVING MONEY, I purchased a 1957, four-door, Chevrolet. I chose a four-door model because I wanted it to be easy for MaMa to get in and out of the car. Since I had a car, I had to chauffeur two of Ketona's legends, Ms. Karrie "Kate Goo" Lancaster and Ms. Maebell Graves. These two ladies lived next door to each other. It was my job to chauffeur them back and forth to the doctor and grocery store. I loved Ms. Maebell, but could not stand for her to get in my car because she smelled just like cigarettes and that smell would get all in my clothes.

Ms. Kate Goo lived on the opposite side of Old Man Reese Davis. She walked like a duck and weighed around three hundred or four hundred pounds. Her clothes were full of patches and she often wore an apron. Her husband would come visit every first of the month and then disappear. She did not worry about a thing because she had all of us. Ms. Kate Goo was a nice lady and she made all of us behave – she believed in discipline. It is funny now, but when Ms. Kate Goo got in the car, the car would lean to one side because of her weight, but I kept my mouth shut and never complained.

Ms. Maebell was a single lady and as I mentioned, she loved to smoke cigarettes. She attended Cedar Grove AME Church with Eula "Cousin Chanky" Avery. Cousin Chanky and Maebell spent a lot of time together sitting on the front porch. Maebell did not have kids. Dot and Doris Jean would do her hair, but really, all of my mama and Cousin Chanky's kids helped Ms. Maebell. Ms. Maebell's house was also near Herman and Rosie Embry, who are the paternal grandparents of Janice, Cheryl and Napoleon Jr.

Mr. Fred and Mrs. Carrie Langford were friends with Ms. Maebell. This couple were some of the pioneers of Cedar Grove. Mr. Fred died from old age, early one Monday morning in the 1950s. He died around the time, the women were washing clothes. His death hurt the community because he was one of our strong leaders, who spoke the truth.

Next door to Fred and Carrie Langford, lived Big P and Ma Trousseau. Ma Trousseau's daughter was Bessie. Bessie's son was Dimples. Dimples ended up marrying Doll Walker. This family was close to Ms. Maebell and Ms. Kate Goo. Big P and Ma Trousseau later moved to Milwaukee, WI. After moving there, Big P opened a barber shop. Someone robbed Big P's barbershop and killed him. When word got back to Ketona that our Big P was dead, we just could not believe it. It is sad when devastating events happen to those you love and respect because all of us know Big P was a large man, but he would never bring harm to anyone.

MS. INEZ' COMPANION WAS DOC GREEN. They lived on Long Street across from the Glasgow family. When you visited Ms. Inez, Doc Green would come out the backroom to greet you. No one in Ketona will ever forget Doc Green! Doc Green had a temper and was a convicted murderer.

He bragged about serving prison time on Alcatraz Island. One time, he got mad at his sister, Ms. Jesse and her boys and shot at their house on Pine Hill Road. When he fired the gun, everybody ran out like flies. Even in Doc Green's old age, he made the newspaper for shooting at someone. You did not play with Doc Green. Doc Green would be kind to you if you were kind to him, but if you disrespected him, you better start running because he would shoot.

Next door to the Glasgow's home on Long Street were Albert and Fannie Devers. Fannie was known as Ma Fannie and she raised Ronald and Samuel "Sam" Brewster. Ronald and Sam's sister was Bonnie and she lived with their grandmother, Alice Grant. Samuel "Tootie" Brewster, Sr. and Queen Esther Brewster Embry were the parents of Ronald, Sam, and Bonnie. Sam became a baseball star while attending Miles College and is now listed in their Hall of Fame.

Albert Devers started the first little league baseball team in Ketona. He took the time to show all of us how to play baseball the right way. He was a good coach. Ma Fannie was the housekeeper for the Chief of Police for Tarrant City and she was the sister to Granny. Ma Fannie kept all the ladies updated with the latest gossip, she would hear from the white folks down in Tarrant City. This is how Ketona kept up with what was happening away from our two streets and one road.

THE SUPERSTAR OF KETONA was Sammy C. Williams. He was from Ketona and played for minor league baseball teams. Sammy C. lived in San Jose, California. His siblings were Warren G., Fleter "Ms. Boot", Bunchie, Louie "Skinny" and Puddin. Sammy C. was the cousin to Bob Williams. When Sammy C. would fly home to visit Ketona, everyone got excited because he had style and he was our superstar.

All of us would come outside when word got out that Sammy C. was home in Ketona! We all wanted to see what he would be wearing. Sammy C. always would get out the car with grace and flash a smile. All of us would leave our front porch and move towards Sammy C.

Sammy C. would take time to talk to each one of us and tell us all about what he saw all over the world. Our Sammy C. made it and made us feel like we were right there with him. One thing, I can say about Sammy C. is that although he achieved fame, he never ever forgot about little Ketona.

Sammy C.'s sister, Puddin married George Whatley. George Whatley died around 1984. George Whatley often wore a white cap and was a sharp dresser.

George Whatley's parents were Charlie Whatley and Mattie Payne Whatley. Ma Mattie had Arthur, Robert, Willie, and Bertha before she married Charlie. Mama Mattie's mother was Granny Jenkins. The Whatley family attended Ebenezer with Mama Mattie.

SOME OF THE OLDEST BLACK NEIGHBORHOODS in our area are Maple Grove and Zion City. Those neighborhoods were around way before everyone started moving to Ketona. Before Rushing Spring Baptist Church was built, the Goins, Bates, Woods and a lot of them from Rushing

Spring attended church at Mt. Zion Baptist located in Zion City.

My Paw-Paw was Wesley "Lee" Avery. Paw-Paw's membership was at Mt. Zion Baptist and his funeral was held there. I may have been around the age of five years old when he died and I remember going to Paw-Paw's funeral. After Paw-Paw died, MaMa, Harold, Pat, and I attended Rushing Spring Baptist Church.

I became a member of Rushing Spring when I was a teenager. I joined during revival along with Dorothy Goodgame Johnson, Phyllis Stewart, Tom Avery, and Rufus Goodgame. We all were baptized over at Five Mile Creek by Rev. Herron. The church had the baptismal pool put in during the late 1950s. After we were baptized, Harold, Charles Jr., and Perry Coleman soon joined Rushing Spring and they were baptized in the new baptismal pool.

I must tell you about Johnny Clark, who was short in stature and medium brown, but the man loved Rushing Spring Baptist Church. He lived in Ketona and was a strong Deacon at Rushing Spring. Deacon Clark lived with Priscilla Jones. Ms. Priscilla owned the home, Doc Smitty later purchased. Before Doc Smitty purchased this home, he rented the house you know as Josephine Graves' home. Coloreda was Josephine's daddy and he would rent the house out to people when he was alive.

If you look at some of the older papers for the church, you will see Deacon Clark's name. Deacon Clark did not sing and pray, but he would help handle business around the church. He always sat to the right in the amen corner on the back pew. All the Deacons sat over there in the amen corner. Deacon Clark sat in the same seat until he died.

Wait, just thought of something, Deacon Clark was also in charge of the Rushing Spring cemetery and would make sure the graves were ready for burial. If anyone from Ketona or Rushing Spring needed to use the cemetery to bury their loved one, you had to go directly to Deacon Clark.

One Saturday, during the 1940s, Deacon Clark was up at the cemetery burning debris. When he left the cemetery, he thought the debris fire was all the way out, but it was not. The entire hill near the church caught afire and the fire came down to the front steps of the Rushing Spring Baptist Church. Mama Shelly, Papa Alec, Cousin Charles, Tom, Charles Jr., Deacon Clark and really just about everyone in Ketona and Rushing Spring went to work putting out the fire.

Together, the community put out the fire as one family unit. That shows you how much we love our church and community. Everybody was working fast, passing the water from the spring near the church. Tears were running down the faces of almost everyone and everyone kept passing the water. Deacon Clark was a quiet man and you could see on his face that he felt so bad about the fire. Everyone reminded him the fire was not intentional. When the fire was out, he had to sit down on the steps to catch his breath and compose himself.

A lady by the name of Estelle "Stelle" Amos, who was married to Dave Amos, purchased Rev. Herron's office furniture that is still at the old church and the pulpit furniture. Cousin Stelle purchased the furniture in the early 1950s. Cousin Stelle was an active, real quiet member at Rushing Spring, but she would give all the money she had to help the church.

Cousin Stelle worked as a maid for the white families in Tarrant City. She became a bad diabetic and had both legs amputated, but she never stopped giving to Rushing Spring. The day Cousin Stelle died, the kids were getting off the bus in front of Cousin Charles' home. Someone yelled, "Cousin Stelle dead, she is dead!"

Every child on the bus ran so fast because no one wanted to lose our Cousin Stelle. Everyone was hollering and then other families ran outside, then all of the families from Rushing Spring were in Ketona at Cousin Stelle's home on Long Street. Cousin Stelle's legacy taught us to be humble. She always taught us the importance of giving even when you do not have too much money. Cousin Stelle was not a relative, but we truly loved her.

Cousin Stelle's mother was Aunt Ida. Aunt Ida was related to Ms. Inez and she was best friends with Jenny Brewster Murray. Aunt Ida was not a relative, but she treated all the kids like an aunt.

Every morning, Aunt Ida cooked breakfast for our 1st grade teacher, Ms. Capers. Students would take turns to pick up Ms. Caper's hot breakfast from Aunt Ida's home. Aunt Ida prepared her breakfast every day because Ms. Capers had to get up early and catch rides to work in Ketona.

Aunt Ida later married Henderson Correthers. Mr. Correthers bought a Mercury car, it was a 1940s model. All of a sudden, he decided to stop driving. He then parked his car inside his barn located in his backyard. Years later, in the 1950s, he decided to tear the barn down and Mr. Correthers' car was sitting in there still looking brand new.

Now over in Rushing Spring, Will Simpson lived next door in a double tenant house right by Papa Alec and Mama Shelly. When Sue and Napoleon Sr. first married, they lived on one side of Mr. Will's house and soon after living there, Janice, their oldest child was born. I would go by and help get the wood to start the fire in the morning to keep the baby warm. I helped bring in the wood because Napoleon Sr. had to work.

Again, this is just another example of how everybody looked out for each other.

Noonie lived near Mama Shelly with her kids, Annette, Michael, Redmond, Alonzo, Edward, and Robert. This family loved Mama Shelly and was part of Rushing Spring Baptist Church. Noonie was a single parent and when I married Vivian, we took a special interest in Noonie's children, in addition to raising our own children, Daryl and LaShawn.

Aunt Lozzie lived in a double tenant house near Papa Alec and Mama Shelly. Aunt Lozzie moved into the home after Aunt Bell died. Everybody loved Aunt Lozzie because she spoke her mind. She did not hold anything on her chest. Aunt Lozzie kept a boyfriend, but she kept her business to herself. You did not want to get out of line with Aunt Lozzie because she was so strong that she could whip a man.

When I was a boy, every Sunday, Aunt Lozzie and other ladies at Rushing Spring would give me a piece of fatback to keep me quiet during church. I would get under the pew and chew that fatback. The ladies would be stumping their feet and having a good old fashion church, but I was enjoying my fatback.

Aunt Lozzie was really a godmother to all of us. She did not have kids so she made time for us. When she died, it hurt badly. Reality set in and it was like we got to go to church and with no Aunt Lozzie. That was an adjustment for Rushing Spring.

MY MOTHER ALONG WITH ME, PAT AND HAROLD lived in the same house with MaMa and Paw-Paw. Paw-Paw's home was built with wood given by Fred Black. Paw-Paw helped build his own home.

In 1948, my mother married Ishmael "Ish" Shelton. Since our family was about to grow with more siblings, MaMa sold Ish, the lot next door to her home and it was on the opposite side of Granny's home. Ish was able to get wood to build the house from two white men named Mr. Richardson and Mr. Harris. Mr. Richardson owned Richardson Hardware, which is still open today in Tarrant City. Mr. Harris co-owned Harris and Smith Clothing Store. These men let Ish tear down one of their homes. Ish taught me how to use a hammer and crowbar to tear down the house. He even took time to show me how to remove the nails from the lumber.

When we started building, Chrisell Turnbow showed me how to complete carpentry work inside the home. Then, Papa Murray taught me how to properly wire our house. Right now, the house is still standing at 615 Pine Hill Road. That house was able to comfortably hold our parents, me, Pat, Harold, Jackie, Ishmael (Bay-Man), Janis, Lawrence (Donnie), and Edna.

THE MEN OF KETONA taught me how to use my hands to WORK! All men need to go to WORK! Ketona did not raise me to be a lazy man. The men of Ketona demonstrated that a man should get out of bed and work to take care of his family. The skills I learned from the men in Ketona prepared me to work for American Cast Iron Pipe Company (ACIPCO). My first day of the job was July 24, 1958.

My role at ACIPCO was serving as a Kneeling-over Operator, so basically I "cooked" pipe. Cousin Charles also worked and retired from ACIPCO. I worked there at ACIPCO, a total of forty-three years and eight months. I happily retired in 2002, but I am thankful because the job allowed me to support my family.

I thank God all of the time for Ketona and Rushing Spring. Our village helped me to excel and do well in life. The Ketona community taught me to serve God and to help somebody. I am forever thankful that the men of Ketona taught me about hard work.

I REMEMBER IN 1967, I had a car accident right there in Ketona. I was on my way driving to Hooper City and hit the telephone pole on the corner near Ebenezer Baptist Church. Once I hit the pole, I got the wind knocked out of me and my eyelid was split open. I also received a cut across my nose. My brother, Harold came to the accident scene and once he saw I was unconscious, he lost it. Harold kept hitting me and telling me to "Bro, wake up!" Soon, I regained consciousness. Harold was hitting me so hard that Ms. LeeAnna told him, "Stop Harold, you stop!"

Ms. Alice and Ms. LeeAnna got all of the glass out of my eye. Everyone around me was panicking because of all the blood coming from my eye and nose. Ms. Alice said, "Y'all it is okay, calm down, Bro has to bleed, so infection won't be so bad on him." Once I got checked out by the doctor, I went to church that Sunday and started singing for Lord. I have been singing now for over fifty years. I am known for singing, "Old Landmark."

WHEN I LEAVE THIS EARTH, I want my grandbaby, Little Vivian to know she has brought so much love and joy into my life. That little girl keeps me going. I expect Little Vivian to watch the company she keeps, and be humble. Little Vivian is named for her paternal grandmother and one trait I want her to have like my wife is to keep up with your family and be a good example. Little Vivian better not worry about keeping up with the crowd, just live by God's Holy Word.

It is important for Little Vivian to use the gifts God blesses her with to minister to God's people. Little Vivian, I want you to be a servant for the Lord – it is so important to work for the Lord. It is my prayer that whatever work, Little Vivian does at Rushing Spring Baptist Church, she should please God and be known for doing what is right and keeping the peace.

It is my prayer for Daryl, LaShawn, Paul, Annette, Justin, Taneisha, and all of my grandchildren to always hold Rushing Spring Baptist Church close to their hearts. I truly love all of you and hold on to our precious memories. Please always remember the teachings of Jesus Christ.

Chapter 10

---

729 Pine Hill Road

"Only talk to no more than two of my children for the book. You might want to use Dot and Charles Jr. One thing, I like about my Dot is she can save a dollar and keep a secret. When she comes to town, she is going to make sure I have fried corn and chicken wings. When I am gone, Dot has to step up and keep my children together." – Charles D. Avery, Sr.

MY NAME IS DOROTHY "DOT" AVERY HUMPHREYS and I grew up at 729 Pine Hill Road located in Ketona. My parents named me after our neighbor, Mama Spencer's daughter, Dorothy, who died; I believe she died at an early age. Our home was a white, A-frame, double tenant home, with a large front porch located right by the train tracks. Our front porch always had chairs and swings for everyone to sit on. We all gathered at the front porch with our family, neighbors and friends.

A total of nine people consistently lived inside our home. It was Daddy, Mudear, me, my sisters, Doris Jean, Carolyn, my brothers, Tom and Charles Jr., my maternal grandmother, Mama Jenny and step-grandfather, Papa Murray. In addition to the nine of us, someone was always spending the night at our home because Mama Jenny had eight children, who visited all the time along with their children.

Mama Jenny was the mother to Willie, Vivian, Jack, Walter (Skeet), Milton (Milt), Olivia, Roy, my mama, and the baby girl was Jenny B. Mama Jenny helped raise Joe Stewart, Ellis "Doc Smitty" Smith and Major Glasgow, and she considered them her sons. This is why we considered them to be just like uncles. 729 Pine Hill Road was always crowded with people and then sometimes Mama Jenny would let boarders live at our home. If you needed a place to stay, Mama Jenny would say, "Come on in." I will tell anybody that I had one of the best childhoods and there was never a dull moment in our home.

ALL OF US LIVED on one side of our home and my grandparents lived on the other side. On our side of the home, my parents slept in the front bedroom, the girls slept in one bed in the middle bedroom, and my brothers shared one bed in the back bedroom of our home. On the other side of the house, Mama Jenny and Papa Murray shared one bedroom. In my grandparents' bedroom, we had a stove that was used to heat the house. My brothers had to add wood and coal to keep it hot.

Another large heater was on the opposite side of the house to warm up our side of the house. Sometimes the house would get so cold, my brothers could blow a cloud of smoke from their mouth because it was not much heat in back of the house. Tom and Charles Jr. had to bundle up close together to keep warm.

Before our family started growing, a border by the name of Josie Hardy lived in the back room and she died back there in 1942. We did not know her, but always heard stories about her. Some in the family called her Aunt Josie and others said Cousin Josie. Aunt Josie's father was Nelson Hardy from Tuscaloosa, AL.

As a child, Charles Jr. use to be scared to go to the back bedroom when he was told someone died back there. He would get so scared that he did not want to get the blankets out of the closet in the back room because he thought Aunt Josie's ghost would jump at him. Charles Jr. would say, "I can't go back there, it's a monkey in the closet." It was no monkey, but he was scared!

Growing up, we had an outdoor toilet in the back yard along with a chicken coot. Papa built our outdoor toilet. On the back porch, we had a #3 washtub and shower that we used to wash our body each day. There was a hole in the floor of the back porch for the water to drain out of the shower and the water would drain onto the ground up under our home. Also, on the back porch was a white, wringer washing machine. We had to manually put our clothes in the wringer and used the rub board to scrub the excess dirt from our clothes.

After washing, we had to hang our clothes on the clothes line in the backyard to dry. Whenever, it was about to rain, all of us would run outside to gather our clothes from the clothes line and we would hang the clothes up inside wherever we could until the rain stopped. In later years, we would go to the laundromat in Tarrant City to wash and dry our clothes.

The county added sewer and gas lines in Ketona around the 1950s. When the gas line was put in, Daddy got rid of the open fireplace in the front of the house. The entire house was remodeled in the 1960s and we ended up with one entry door and our home was no longer a double tenant home.

For a long time, in our kitchen, we had a white, pot belly stove and wood had to be added to keep it hot. We received an electric stove in the 1940s. We did not have a refrigerator because when I was a kid, everyone used an ice box to keep the food cold. Each week, the ice man delivered several pounds of ice to our home. During the 1950s, they started advertising on television, the newer model stoves and refrigerators. When Mudear saw the commercial, Daddy had to go and buy it and upgrade our kitchen.

Before we had our own telephone line, the neighbors had a party-line phone system. Four households would be on the same party line. Our party line consisted of Lucille Avery, my family, a white family on Ketona Road, and another family. You had to wait your turn to use the phone. When you really needed to use the phone, you would say, "Excuse me, can I please use the phone?" The person on the other end, would soon end their telephone conversation. Our telephone number always ended with 4963.

Daddy always kept us with updated versions of the Funk & Wagnalls Encyclopedias and Reader's Digest books in the living room on a book shelf. All of the neighborhood kids would use our encyclopedias to complete their school work. Our dining room would look like a library with everyone being quiet while studying and writing. Daddy never turned anyone away when they were in need of our encyclopedias, but no one could remove the encyclopedias from our home. Our dining table had long benches for everyone to sit on. Even when Daddy died, our encyclopedias were still on the book shelf.

Also, in the living room, we had a large television. Mudear and Daddy always allowed neighbors to come in and watch television. If the neighbors were not watching television at our home, they could go up the street to Cousin Lucille's home. We loved watching Amos and Andy, Sergeant Friday, Boston Blackie, Search for Tomorrow, I Love Lucy, Monday Night Boxing, and Pabst Blue Ribbon was a famous commercial. Families from the neighborhood always had a good time at our home watching television. We would all gather in the living room with our snacks and just enjoy each other's company. During the Monday night boxing match, Daddy placed the television in the front window, in order for everyone to see the boxing match. Our front yard would be filled with our neighbors.

Ms. Maebell never missed coming to our house to watch Sergeant Friday. When it was time for the "Arthur Godfrey Show", Cousin Stelle would come inside because she was not going to miss this television show. Cousin Stelle always brought with her peanut butter candy or orange slices candy.

Mudear was primarily a housewife and a strict disciplinarian. She only worked just a few days down to the laundromat. Although, Mudear was strict, she allowed us to have fun. She did not allow bad behavior and talking back. If we got out of line, Mudear, whipped our butt. She would tell us, "You will not cut up. You will act right." When we visited someone for dinner and if they asked if we wanted a second serving of food, Mudear taught us to say, "No, thank you."

ONE DAY, MUDEAR'S FRIEND, Ms. Dollie, who lived in the ACIPCO neighborhood invited all of us over for dinner. Ms. Dollie and Mudear met at A.H. Parker High School while taking sewing classes together. After eating dinner, Ms. Dollie served everyone ice cream. Ms. Dollie asked, "Kids, do you want some more ice cream?" We responded, "Yes, please." Mudear gave us a look like, "I know you did not!"

When we finished eating ice cream, some of us hit the spoon against the bowl like we wanted more and we could see the anger in Mudear's face because we were acting like we were not use to eating ice cream. When we left Ms. Dollie's home and drove across the railroad tracks to get to our home, Mudear whipped us from the front door to the back door because she taught us to never beg and overeat at someone's home. While whipping us, Mudear said, "Folks ask out of courtesy, not for y'all to beg." After that whipping, we never, ever did that again.

WHILE LIVING AT HOME, we always ate breakfast together as a family at our kitchen table and dinner at the dining room table. Before we ate as a family, Daddy said the same grace all of my life. We would all bow our heads, close our eyes, and Daddy would say, "Oh gracious Father, we thank you for the food that we are about to receive for the nourishment of our body for Christ sake." Together, as a family, we said, "Amen." Our weekly Sunday breakfast consisted of chicken with gravy, rice, grits, biscuits, and eggs. I loved to eat the breast of the chicken and so did Mudear and Tom. We had to create a weekly rotating schedule on who would eat the breast of the chicken.

Our mother attended Cedar Grove AME Church and all of us kids attended Rushing Spring with Daddy. When we walked to church, Daddy had us in a line and we looked like a group of ducks walking down the road. Once we arrived to Rushing Spring, Mama Shelly and Papa would join us to walk up the hill for church. Even though Mudear did not attend church with us, she demanded us to sit down and be quiet in church. We all knew if we broke the rule, she would know by the time we arrived home.

It was mandatory that all of us take food to those less fortunate. If someone was walking the train tracks and they appeared to be hungry, one of us immediately took them food to eat. If a neighbor, called and needed food, without hesitation, we walked to their home and took them food. If someone was sick or elderly, we provided them food. When our Uncle Verbin was in college, Daddy provided weekly groceries for his family because they lived up the street and later moved to Zion City.

We were fortunate because Daddy's job at ACIPCO had a commissary where we could buy, food, clothes, toys and other household items. If he did not have the cash to pay for our items, he could have the money taken out of his paycheck. There were times when we had to buy so much, that he had a very small paycheck. When we were kids, Daddy made a little over $1.00 per hour, but we did not miss a beat.

When we were out of high school, he made over $2.70 per hour. There were times, Mudear would sew our dresses, but we were always clean with nice clothing. Mudear always had fancy hats to wear on Sunday. She and Cousin Mattie Pearl were known in Ketona for their fancy, Sunday hats. Daddy always gave his paycheck to Mudear and together they performed miracles with little money.

If any of asked for a new outfit, Mudear would tell Daddy, we needed to go to the downtown shopping district in Birmingham. All of shopped at Loveman's, Pizitz, Odum Bowers and White, New Ideal, J.J. Newberry and there were other available stores.

Before we got new bikes, Tom and Charles Jr. would take old parts and make bikes. During the month of December in the 1950s, Daddy bought us new bikes. My bike was silver and red with a radio on the handle bars. As Charles Jr. was carrying his bike home, he said, "Daddy, how is Santa bringing bikes to our home and we are carrying our bikes home?" Daddy laughed and had to tell us the truth about Santa Claus.

Doris Jean did not want a bike because she just wanted to dance. Doris Jean won any dance contest that came through Tarrant City and Hooper City. She was also crowned Ms. Hooper City High School. All of us are much older than our younger sister, Carolyn. Carolyn is very studious and very smart.

On Friday afternoons, the ladies of the neighborhood would come to our home so Mudear could shampoo and style their hair. The ladies would sit in the kitchen because Mudear had to use the stove to heat up the straightening comb. If the ladies just needed their hair braided, we would sometimes sit on the front porch. Mudear would sometimes make Doris Jean and I braid the older ladies hair. Mudear finished cosmetology school after graduating from Hooper City High School.

We always had animals at our home. In the backyard, Daddy always kept a hunting dog. We had cats, chickens and ducks in our pond that was located in the backyard. We got rid of the ducks in the 1950s. Daddy kept one cow on our land in Rushing Spring for our milk and butter. All of us loved our cow named Daisy.

Daddy was an avid hunter and he was known for not missing his target. When Verbin Jr. lived in Zion City, Daddy made an effort to always take him hunting in Rushing Spring with him and Papa. One time, Mama Shelly said, "Charles, I bet you can't shoot that jack rabbit." Daddy said, "Watch me." Daddy shot the rabbit, with the first shot. Daddy just laughed because he knew would hit his target.

Everyone in the house knew not to bother Daddy's guns. There were times the sheriff would bring the Ku Klux Klan on our street. Daddy would make everyone get under the dining room table. He would stand behind the front door with his shotgun, just in case they entered. As we grew older, we all learned how to hold and shoot a shotgun. His words to us were, "If anyone enters our home to kill us, we must shoot to kill. We will not be afraid."

As kids, every weekend, our parents would let our cousins and friends spend the night. Sam Jr. and David stayed at our home on the weekend. Some weekends, Aunt Odell and Aunt Lottie Mae spent the night after partying down in Tarrant City. Daddy could hear his sisters talking and giggling while walking home at night on the train tracks to go to Rushing Spring. He would go outside and say, "Y'all come inside my house, it is too late to walk home." Aunt Odell and Aunt Lottie Mae would jump in bed with me and my sisters. When we had a lot of company, we slept on our rollaway beds and let the company use our beds. Mudear made sure we were always hospitable to our guests.

OUR COUSINS, VIVIAN AVERY AND PERRY COLEMAN spent a lot of time with us. Although, they were our cousins, we considered them to be our sister and brother. Perry was there every day because he would wait at our house until his mom got off work. When Aunt Lottie Mae got off work, they would walk together to Rushing Spring because they lived with Mama Shelly and Papa. We missed Perry, when they moved with his father to Germany. When Perry got back to Ketona from Germany, he was over six feet tall. We could not believe, he would ever be that tall.

Vivian was Uncle Verbin and Aunt Lois' oldest daughter. Vivian spent most of her time with Aunt Lois' oldest sister, Ms. Geneva. Ms. Geneva brought Vivian to our home on Friday's to spend the weekends. We would walk to Long Street with Vivian and spend time with Aunt Lois, Shirley and Verbin Jr.

Ms. Geneva brought Vivian to Ketona because she had to work on the weekends. She sold Watkins products, meaning she had products for your cakes, spices, and health remedies. Mudear always bought her baking products from Ms. Geneva. On Sunday, Mudear would get Vivian ready for church, just like she did for us. Mudear would give Vivian fresh towels for her bath, press her hair and iron her clothes. After ironing, Mudear would hang up Vivian's Sunday dress along with our dresses. Vivian loved going to Rushing Spring. She would look up and Daddy and say, "Uncle Charles, let's go to Rushing Spring." We would hold hands and be happy walking together. As we walked everyone was happy Vivian was with us in Ketona. We loved our Vivian, she was an angel!

When Vivian took ill, Daddy had Mr. Augustus to pick him up from our home. Daddy and Augustus drove to Montgomery, Alabama where Uncle Verbin was living at a house while attending Alabama State University. I can remember someone saying, "They made it back to

Birmingham with Verbin." Our phone started ringing, in the middle of the night and Mudear screamed and told us, "Vivian is dead!" We all jumped up and ran to Mudear. Everybody at 729 Pine Hill Road, screamed and cried, we could not stop crying. We were screaming, "No, not Vivian! Oh Vivian!"

When the Friday after Vivian's death rolled around and it was no Vivian coming thru the door, we cried some more. Vivian was one sweet child. She was so intelligent, courteous and obedient. She had a heart of love and when she would see us, she would get so excited and we would too. Like I have said before, Vivian was much more than a first cousin, she was truly like a sister. Vivian left us at the age of ten years old in April 1953.

Mudear was always crazy about Uncle Rec's wife, Aunt Kate. Aunt Kate would come by the house with both of her girls, Jackie and Gwen. After Vivian died, the next month, Uncle Rec's daughter, Jackie died in May 1953.

When Jackie took ill, Daddy took our household every day to sit for a little while with Jackie up until she died. Jackie did not know we were in the room. She was in bed and not responding. Jackie's eyes were closed and Aunt Kate was right by her side.

I remember all of us looking at each other not saying a word, then we would get sad staring at Jackie. When Jackie died, we were still dealing with Vivian's death. We loved Jackie and it hurt us when she died. We all felt sorry for Gwen because losing Jackie meant she would not have a sibling in the house. Vivian and Jackie's deaths were so close together and no Avery will ever forget the year of 1953. Jackie and Vivian are both buried at Shadowlawn.

IN 1959, MAMA JENNY DIED. A few hours before she died, a hobo was walking the train tracks, dressed in black. We took food to the hobo. All of a sudden, the hobo disappeared. Daddy said, "Go out there and tell the hobo to not go down the train tracks right now because Tarrant City Police will put him in jail." We looked all over for the hobo. In the midst of not finding him Mama Jenny had a terrible cough and soon died.

The funeral home soon came to pick up Mama Jenny's body. Before the funeral, she was brought back into our home and her body remained overnight in our living room. All of her descendants and neighbors sat in our living room to give their final goodbyes.

Her funeral took place across the street at Cedar Grove. Mama Jenny had an impact on many people and that was one sad funeral. Mudear and all her siblings sobbed profusely. Every man that Mama Jenny raised could not control their tears. Mama Jenny is buried in Village Springs next to her sister, Minnie. Both of them have concrete slabs over their graves.

PART 3
THE JOURNEY

Chapter 11

Life and Death

"Charles Jr. and Harold never knew the word, 'defeat'. Together, they always acted as one team. I admired their strength and I want Charles Jr. to remember, he will never, ever be defeated when leading God's people. Tell Charles Jr. when it looks like he is down for the count, God will raise him above the enemy. – Charles D. Avery, Sr.

HAROLD BOOKER AND I did not share the same mother and father, but we were just like brothers. Harold had a bad temper and I was the one, who tried to keep the peace when possible. If Harold got into a disagreement with anyone, I had to calm him down or we had to do what was necessary to protect each other. In high school, Harold was around 5 feet 8 inches and 110 pounds. I was 117 pounds and 5 feet 7 inches. We were considered small and short, but we were respected by everyone. Mama Shelly would give us goat milk to fatten us up, but it did not work. Harold and I were determined that no one would disrespect and run over us because of our size.

My brother and buddies closest to me always called me, "Dank". While attending class at Hooper City High School, someone yelled at me and said, "Dank, somebody messing with Doris Jean." The teacher would not let me leave class to check on my sister. Doris Jean and I acted as though we were twins and I always protected my sister. The teacher yelled at us to sit down and would not let me leave the classroom. Harold looked at me and said, "Dank, Let's go!" Together, we jumped out the class window to make sure my sister was okay.

Harold and I were some of the best football players that hit the football field at Hooper City High School. My classmates will tell you that I was one of the fastest running backs on the football team and Harold was one of the best kickers from our school district. I was determined that I would outrun anyone that tried to catch me. Even when someone was about to tackle me, I could hear Harold say, "Go Dank, Go!" I would run so fast, I could feel the wind hitting my face. My cousin, Carl Turnbow will tell you, "Dank was a bad boy on the football field."

During our senior year in high school, four, stellar students from Ketona decided to have our names placed on the election ballot for senior class officer positions. We were determined to win and yes, we won! We had no doubt that we would win! Brenda Faye Avery won the Secretary position. Delores Correthers won the position of Treasurer. Harold Booker won the position of Vice President and I, Charles D. Avery, Jr. proudly won the position of Senior Class President. When we arrived home after Election Day, the Ketona community was excited because the four of us won by a landslide. Little did we know, Hooper City High

School was about to make history during the Civil Rights Movement as the last school to demonstrate in the streets of downtown Birmingham.

I was very aware of the Civil Rights Movement because my father always took our household downtown to participate in mass meetings. Daddy took a chance in taking us because if his job found out he was participating in the mass meetings, he would immediately be fired. You could feel the presence of God at the mass meetings. Everyone in the building acted as one family. One song that stands out from the mass meetings is "Ain't Gonna Let Nobody Turn me Round"........I can hear the singing now. We as a family would stand up and sing to the top of our lungs.

One night while attending a mass meeting, we got to see and hear Dr. King speak. When Dr. King rose to the podium, everyone in attendance was shouting and thanking God for our leader. I can honestly say, at that moment, a feeling came all over my body. I was almost shaking because it was like I knew God was calling me to make a difference and I was ready to make a difference. Everyone attending the mass movements motivated each other because we were determined that fear would not keep us away from demonstrating to promote change to end segregation and to obtain equal rights.

Before we heard the voice of Dr. King, Daddy motivated us to never accept *no* for an answer. When we were coming up, black people had to take a test to vote. Daddy decided it was time for him to go before the judge and take the voting test.

The judge asked Daddy, "Nigger, tell me how high is high?" Next, the judge said, "Now, Nigger, tell me how many bubbles are in a bar of soap."

The first time Daddy took the test, he became frustrated and left. Our Daddy went right back and tried to give scientific responses to the judge's questions.

The judge gave Daddy his right to vote, but he then made it even more difficult for Daddy, so he thought. The judge chose Cullman, AL as Daddy's voting location instead of Tarrant, AL where we lived. You can go online and read about the racial tension in Cullman, AL. Daddy did not let his voting location stop him from voting for every election. Cullman was approximately fifty miles from our home. Due to the racial tension in Cullman, Daddy always had a male neighbor to ride with him. If my Daddy was willing to risk his life to vote, I knew I had to march!

I believe it was the first Monday of May 1963; a lady by the name of Mrs. Annie Peterson came to our school to recruit students to demonstrate. When Harold and I got off the bus that morning, someone came to me and said, "You are the Senior Class President and someone is here to speak to you. Go to the office." I did not know what was going on and I told Harold to come with me. When I arrived at the office, my homeroom teacher, Mrs. Lucille Ayers told me, "This is Mrs. Annie Peterson and I need you to listen to her."

Mrs. Annie Peterson greeted me and said, "All other schools are already marching, but Hooper City High School is my school and this school has not marched. The jails are filling up and this is the only school left for me to recruit from. Charles Avery, the Civil Rights Movement needs Hooper City High School." Mrs. Ayers smiled and nodded her head at me. I looked at both ladies and said, "You bet!" When I left the office, Harold and I walked out the back door.

Our principal, Mr. William Jackson was totally against our school participating in demonstrations. Mr. Jackson called the sheriff on Mrs. Peterson. Mrs. Peterson was escorted away from the school and I witnessed it with my own eyes.

The word went out throughout the school, that we were about to march into downtown Birmingham. The elementary school was located on the Hooper City school campus. Before I took my position to rally the students, I thought of Daddy because if I was put in jail, he would possibly lose his job. My family needed Daddy's income to survive. However, Daddy always said, "You do not worry about my job, make your own decision." I believe deep down in his heart, he wanted me to march.

As I approached the top of the steps, I could feel the Holy Spirit. I took my position in front of the mass crowd. I had no time to think about getting butterflies in my stomach. I was looking at a sea of students from the first through the twelfth grade. Harold smiled and said, "Go Dank!" Harold was ready!

As I stood on top of the steps, I took off my sports coat and twirled it over my head. I repeatedly yelled, "Let's Go, Hooper City! Let's Go! We can do this!" I jumped down from the stairs and spoke to the football team. It was decided for the football players to line up on each side of the young kids. My cousin, Carl Turnbow from Ketona was one of the football players, who protected the small kids. Harold and I were in the front of the line.

When all of us made it to Village Creek, sheriffs with batons were waiting on us. The sheriffs asked, "Who is leading this march?" The students pointed their fingers at me and said, "He is!" As the sheriffs made their way toward Harold and me, a lady came off her porch and yelled, "Don't hit him!" Once she grabbed us and escorted us to her porch, the students started running everywhere. This lady, who we did not know opened the front door of her shotgun house and said, "Run as fast as you can!" Harold and I kept running until we reached 16th Street, which was near Village Creek.

Once we arrived to 16th Street, we saw our school bus, we knew it was our school bus because it had the number twenty-one painted on it. The bus driver saw us and stopped, in order for us to jump on. Harold and I then told the bus driver that students from Hooper City High School are scattered everywhere. He said, "I will find them." The bus driver then dropped us at Sixteenth Street Baptist Church.

Before I entered the church, I saw Uncle Rec. Uncle Rec was always involved in the Civil Rights Movement and his photo was featured on the front cover of Times Magazine on May 4, 1963. Uncle Rec was fired from his job at U.S. Pipe due to that photo being published. Uncle Rec's daughter, Gwen was attending college at Hampton University and he did not need to lose his job.

As I got closer to Uncle Rec, I yelled, "Uncle Rec!" He said, "Boy, does your Daddy know you are down here?" I said, "Uncle Rec, tell them to send more buses to find students from Hooper City. The students are everywhere!" Uncle Rec walked Harold and me up the steps of the church. He told the staffers to send additional buses to find the kids.

When Harold and I entered the church, classes were going on about nonviolence and what to expect when we went back outside. The staffers then lined us up to go outside of the church. Before we could march again, the sheriffs had the paddy wagons parked waiting on us. Luckily, Harold and I were on the same paddy wagon and when we looked up, we saw Dick Gregory. Although we were in the paddy wagon, we started saying, "Dick Gregory, that's you!"

The paddy wagons dropped us off to the Alabama State Fairground. The sheriffs then led us to an open field that was surrounded by barbed wire to ensure we could not leave. Livestock was near this area and some kids were placed inside the barn with the livestock. I remember when it started to rain and this was HARD rain! We had no covering over our heads. When the lightning hit the barbed wire, one girl cried and said, "God does not even love us." Once she said that, we started singing freedom songs and we could then see, the clear blue sky open up.

After the rain stopped, everyone in the holding cells was ordered to board dump trucks. The dump trucks dropped kids off at the County Jail and some went to the City Jail. Harold and I were taken to the City Jail. The jail was overcrowded and we only saw two toilets that were not working. The jail had large fans in the window. Harold and I were shivering from the cold and we were still wet from the rain water.   When it was time to eat, we had to form a line to enter the cafeteria. Ladies with bats would stand around us. Breakfast was served, first thing in the morning; lunch was served at 12:00pm and dinner at 5:00pm. During breakfast, we were served black coffee, apple sauce, grits, fatback, and a hoecake. Sometimes we received a hard biscuit. The ladies served Kool-Aid, apple sauce, corn bread, greens and bologna for lunch. They sometimes served the same meal served during lunch for dinner. Although, we were served food to eat, they did not allow us to eat. As soon as you tried to sit down and eat, they took their bats and hit the table for you to get up and return to the jail cell. We tried to grab food and stuff it in our mouth real quick.

Mr. Dick Gregory was a man sent by God. Although we were all in jail together, he took time to put on a comedy show for us. One night, the jailers took Mr. Gregory outside and beat him. Mr. Gregory came back bloody and even though he had been beaten, he still tried to ease our minds with comedy. This man was in pain, but he did not worry about his pain. His sole focus was to make sure all of us were okay.

Every time, we walked by a window of the jail, we could see my mother, Eula Avery and Harold's mother, Mattie Pearl Shelton. Our mothers would even stand outside in the rain with their dresses to be close to us. Mudear and Mattie Pearl wanted to ensure they were present when we were released from jail. Although the jailers had baseball bats and guns, that would not have stopped our mothers from trying to protect us.

Some of us were initially denied bond and could not be released. We went to jail on a Monday and released on a Friday. I later heard that A. G. Gaston sent the bail money for many of us to be released. I was one of the last ones to be released because the jailer released you by calling your last name in reverse order. Harold's last name started with the letter 'B', but he would not leave the jail until I was released. When we were released from jail, we walked out of jail and locked arms.

Once I returned to school, I was scheduled to give a speech during our graduation commencement ceremony. The principal said, "Charles Avery is no longer speaking at graduation." The principal was mad because I participated in the Civil Rights demonstrations. Mrs. Ayers and Mrs. Jones became angry and went to the principal to speak on my behalf. In the end, I was able to give my speech as the Senior Class President. Even though, I spoke, the principal still made it difficult for me. He would not hand over my high school diploma.

Several weeks after Harold and I went to jail, I was riding in the rear of the bus. I thought Harold would sit by me like always, but he did not. Once Harold got on, he said, "Dank, we have been to jail and I will no longer ride in the back of the bus." As we walked down the steps of the bus, the bus driver kicked Harold in the back. Harold got up off the ground and shouted some obscenities back to the bus driver. Once we arrived home, everyone knew what happened on our bus ride. We knew the Ku Klux Klan would probably come soon to harm us. Mudear bought me a bus ticket to North Chicago to live with my brother. My life changed overnight.

AROUND 1965, MUDEAR WAS VISITING us at Tom and Mary's home in North Chicago. While Mudear was washing dishes, I walked outside to the mailbox. I held in my hand a letter addressed to me from the U.S. Government. I did not open the letter until I got back inside with Mudear. I opened the letter and read it aloud to Mudear. The letter read that I was being drafted into the United States Army to serve in the Vietnam War. When Mudear heard that she screamed and grabbed me. She was sobbing and repeatedly said, "Not my boy! Not my boy!"

Mudear called my sister, Dot and told her I was headed to Vietnam. Dot and her husband, George left Michigan and drove to North Chicago to spend time with me before I was headed to Vietnam. It meant a lot for them to spend the day with me.

When I arrived to Alabama from North Chicago, I went straight home to Ketona. I told Daddy to use my 1963 Chevrolet while I was serving in the U.S. Army. Before I left to report to duty, I went to find Harold. The two of us spent time talking and catching up.

Before leaving, I also spent time with Granny. Granny said, "Charles Jr. when you get over there, I want you to look at the moon every night at 12:00am. No matter where you go, we will both be looking at the same moon together, so every night at 12:00am, we will pray together. Together, we will pray for your safe return back to Ketona." She ended our conversation, by saying, "Charles Jr., I love you."

I spent some time with Harold and my buddies from Ketona before leaving for Montgomery. As I was about to board the bus for Montgomery, Bro and Vivian met me at the bus station and did not leave me until the bus pulled off. In my hand, I had a white bible given to me by my church member, Sister Wessie Howard.

Once I arrived to Montgomery, AL, I had to complete a series of tests. After leaving Montgomery, I reported to Fort Gordon, Georgia. As I got off the bus, I entered a new world that I had never seen or thought of. All around me Sergeants were yelling, "Get down! Get down on the ground! Give me five!" We were then ordered to get haircuts and received our military uniforms. We received training to be the first placement troops for the Vietnam War.

When I arrived in Fort Gordon, I saw several familiar faces reporting to duty. I saw my close friend, Lawrence "Bo" Carson and then I saw my classmate, Robert Johnson from Bradford. I even saw several white guys I knew from Robinwood. I completed basic training, advanced training and jump school with several of these guys. Robert ended up not serving in Vietnam due to an injury. Bo and I completed training together but eventually were separated. Bo served in the 101st Unit and I served in the 173rd Unit.

While in training, we were taught desensitization and dehumanization of the enemy. We had to endure one week of heat acclimatization to prepare for the hot weather in Vietnam. The superiors prepared our minds for war and we were taught to have no compassion. Despite how we were trained, I never put my spirituality to the side.

Every day, Mudear wrote me a letter and always ended my letters with scriptures. Before leaving for Vietnam, I made it a point to sit down and write her a letter every day. Mudear's letters always brought consolation to me and eased my mind. Also, I never forgot to look up at the moon to pray with Granny every night at 12:00am. Even right now, when I look at the moon, I get teary-eyed sometimes because I think of Granny. Mudear saved all of our letters to each other and I still have them.

The first day we arrived in Vietnam and jumped off the helicopters, there was a tree line of gunfire in front of us from the enemy. Our Sergeant said, "Get up off the ground! On line! Shoot! Shoot!" We had just jumped off the helicopter and had to jump right up shooting. People were falling down to the ground on my left and to my right. As men were falling down, I said, "Come on buddy, let's go, get up!" I soon realized these men were dead. Our Sergeants were always behind us giving orders. They were never in front of us giving orders.

The next day, it rained and I pulled out my poncho from my backpack. When I pulled out the poncho, it was shredded with bullet holes. I looked at it and said, "My God!" Other soldiers started pulling out their ponchos and every poncho had bullet holes. This shows you how close we came to death!

I fought every day while serving in Vietnam without changing clothes. While fighting, I remember shooting while carrying the bodies of deceased soldiers. We never left an American soldier behind.

I am sure I had water to drink, but I honestly do not remember ever drinking water. A helicopter would come once per day to drop off a hot meal only if they could safely land without being shot down. The sea-rations we carried in our backpack had a date stamp of 1945. We were actually eating leftover food from World War II.

I remember seeing and walking by the South China Sea. After four or five months of serving my country, I got shot in my right arm on June 9, 1966 around 3:00pm. I was shot in Vũng Tàu near the South China Sea. During the same time I was shot, Daddy felt that something was wrong. My parents told me, Daddy jumped out of bed screaming, "Charles Jr. is in trouble. My boy needs me. Where is my gun?" After screaming, Daddy fainted and fell on the floor in their bedroom.

After being shot, I was medevac by helicopter to the 32nd Infantry Field Hospital. I recall hearing the surgeon say to another doctor, "This soldier will make it. He has a terrible wound and I can save his arm." Once I was awake from anesthesia, the surgeon told me, "Never let anyone else operate on your arm. Your humerus bone in your shoulder was shot up." I looked confused and he had to explain it in a way that I understood. He then said, "I had to reverse the knuckle inside your shoulder to make the bone fit. You will never have full use of your arm, but you have an arm."

After leaving this surgeon, I was sent to different stations for evaluations throughout the country and I never let anyone touch my arm for another surgery. After leaving Vietnam, I was sent to the United States and remained in the hospital for a few weeks. I remained in a body cast and was eventually flown home. Once I got off the airplane, I was placed into a taxi cab driven by a white man. I gave him my address and he drove me directly to Ketona. He almost passed the house and I said, "Wait, you are about to pass my house."

The cab driver did not help me get out of the car, but I was able to get the strength to open the car door. When I opened the door, Ms. Maebell saw me. Ms. Maebell screamed, "Charles Jr.!" Maebell did not have the strength run, but she tried. Then Ronald Brewster's friend saw me and said, "That's Dank!" Ronald and everyone, who was standing on Long Street, ran toward me. They all helped me get out of the car.

Mudear and Daddy were not home when I arrived. Maebell sat on the front porch with me since the house was locked. It was dusk dark when I saw my car with Daddy and Mudear inside. As they were turning into the driveway, they saw me.

Daddy stopped the car and Mudear literally ran to me. Daddy was right behind her trying to get to me. Mudear could not stop hollering as she was running. I know everyone heard Mudear. She too was screaming, "Charles Jr.! Charles Jr!" She kept hugging me and did not want to let me go. Mudear forgot all about me being in a body cast. Daddy looked straight into my eyes and embraced me. Daddy cried and said, "My baby boy." Maebell did not leave the house until they got me in bed.

My parents placed me inside the front bedroom and pulled the curtain back so I could look outside. If it was late at night, my neighbors knocked on my window to wave at me. I remember the next day after I arrived home, a funeral was taking place across the street at Ebenezer. I asked, "Who died?" Mudear said, "Jim Smith from Robinwood was killed in Vietnam." I became emotional because when Jim saw me in the jungle over in Vietnam, he said, "Hey Dank." I was startled and said, "Who is that?" The voice said, "It's me, Jim from Robinwood." We ran towards each other and gave each other a quick embrace and kept fighting. I saw him a few weeks before he was killed.

While I was home, a black fly got in my open wound. We all thought it was a blister. Uncle Major Glasgow came by and looked at my wound. He said, "That is not a blister that is a black fly. You better get him to the hospital before infection takes over."

Eventually, the military sent me to Fort Polk in Louisiana to receive additional medical care. As I was sitting on the steps, I saw the soldiers marching. All of a sudden, a voice said, "Dank, Dank!" I could hear the Sergeant yelling, "Boy, get in line!" Guess who was yelling my name? Harold Booker! Harold yelled back at the Sergeant, "This man is my cousin." Harold sat right there on the step with me for a quick moment and we embraced. He soon left to catch up with his troops. Even though he was still in training, Harold found a way to visit me every day for a few weeks until he was sent to Vietnam.

To me, it seems like Harold served in Vietnam for almost one year. When we were home from Vietnam, neither one of us were right mentally. We both would drink to suppress our thoughts and nightmares, but Harold would drink all day and all night. His mom would call and say, "Charles Jr.

come over here and see about Harold." I was always able to calm him down and make him go to bed. Harold never gave me problems when I went to help him.

I vividly remember the both of us sitting on the front porch praying for our neighbors, who went in after us to serve in Vietnam. Harold prayed and then I prayed for the safe return of our neighbors. Together, we prayed for Doug, Alfred, Ronald, and Carl. Harold and I were proud to learn that my cousin, Carl Turnbow from Long Street, who also served in Vietnam, received the Silver Star. Harold said, "We boys from Ketona ain't scared of no war!" Carl was in a bunker when a sniper attacker inserted an AK-47 rifle into the bunker and sprayed it with automatic weapons, killing three men and seriously wounding other soldiers. Carl forgot about his own safety and assisted in carrying wounded soldiers across 75 meters of open ground to the station to receive aid. The open fire lasted three and a half hours.

Harold died in December 1979 due to heavy drinking. Even though Harold is not physically here with me, I can still feel his presence. I see him in my dreams and I still hear his voice. When I educate others on the Civil Rights Movement, it is like he whispers to me and reminds me what to include in my speech.

I cannot really describe our bond, but it was like we shared a spiritual bond. My paternal great-grandfather was James Manual Avery and Harold's grandfather was Uncle Lee. Harold and I ended up uniting our family because we shared an unbreakable bond, just like our great-grandfathers. Our forefathers were sent here for a reason and then God placed us here to make a difference. It is in our bloodline to be history makers and great leaders.

I MARRIED JERRI YEARS AFTER I had been discharged from the Vietnam War. I am thankful for Jerri because she could sense something was not right with me mentally. Jerri continuously begged me to let the military check me out and I refused over and over. Later I heard others, who served in the military speak about post-traumatic stress syndrome (PTSD). When I heard the symptoms, I then accepted I needed to be checked out. Veteran Affairs was able to provide me the proper treatment and I will forever be grateful to my wife for pushing me to go.

Jerri and I share an unbreakable bond that will never be broken. God sent us to each other. Jerri and I married in 1975 and Jerri loved Harold, just like I did. The first time I saw Jerri, I was at the bar located at the A.G. Gaston Hotel. She was standing by the jukebox and asked for a quarter. I said to Jerri, "I will soon marry you." She said, "I only asked you for a quarter for the jukebox." We ended up talking and the rest is history.

Jerri was instrumental in helping to care for my son, Chuck. When we first married, Jerri and I lived with her parents in Norwood. One morning, Chuck noticed my car in front of the house and had the school van driver to stop. He told the van driver, "That's my daddy's car!" The van driver rang the doorbell and Mother [Jerri's mother] answered the door. The van driver asked, "Does this boy's Daddy live here?" When Mother saw Chuck, she yelled for us to come to the door. After that moment, the van driver brought Chuck to our home every weekday. Chuck had to be around the age of five years old and never told anyone. Chuck was able to see us every morning on his way to school. I will tell anybody that was nobody, but

God that allowed us to see my son on his way to school.

After almost two years of marriage, Jerri and I wanted to hurry up and have a baby. When Jerri became pregnant with Dina, I cannot describe in words the excitement we felt. Jerri called everybody to tell them she was pregnant. I was so happy Jerri was going to be a mother. We both were in our thirties. Every weekend, Chuck and Jerri studied books and kept up with each stage of Dina's development.

From day one, Jerri always said, "I will give birth to only one child." We did not care if we had a boy or girl, we just wanted a healthy baby. When Jerri went into labor, I think we were both overexcited. The doctor told me I could not go into the delivery room if they did not find something to cover my afro because the surgical cap would not fit. The housekeeper then gave me an apron to cover my afro.

When Jerri went into labor with Dina, she fainted due to her blood pressure. I was told that Jerri and Dina may not make it and I had to make a decision. I told the doctor, "Save my wife!" Jerri and Dina both survived. After holding my baby, I knew she would be special. Others even knew something was different about Dina.

After Dina was born, I was watching a television show and the Queen Mother of England was speaking on raising royal children. When I heard her words, it changed my total outlook on how I wanted to raise my children. Mudear taught us to do our very best and I taught my kids that being mediocre will never be an option growing up in our household. We tried to raise our children as though they were royalty. It was mandatory that Chuck and Dina have proper etiquette skills when greeting people and eating at the table. We encouraged them to play tennis and golf. Chuck was always our star athlete. Dina was too sensitive to play sports, but she ended up enjoying golf.

When Dina turned four years old, Dr. Maryann Manning got word about Dina's reading and oratorical skills. Dr. Manning went to visit Dina at Korner Kinder College and then she came to our home for a visit. Dr. Manning wanted to learn how we were able to teach Dina how to read before entering school. I told Dr. Manning, "When Jerri and I get home, we both have a school with her. If I get home late, Dina knows to wait up so we can practice writing words in cursive and print on her Sesame Street blackboard. It is all about taking time with your kids."

She asked us, "How does this child already know how to give speeches?" I responded by saying, "Dina asked me to train her voice to be the best because she wants to speak at churches. Our Youth Department at Rushing Spring teaches all children how to give speeches." Dr. Manning looked at us and said, "Really?" Jerri and I both said, "Yes."

Dina started working at the age of four and Chuck was eleven years old. I had my own business named Sunshine Home Care Services. Several men from Ketona worked for me. Dina was in charge of calling customers to schedule my appointments and logging in all daily receipts. She was also in charge of calling customer if they had an unpaid invoice. Chuck had to help paint houses, clean buildings, and complete lawn care. When Chuck was not in school, he was with me working.

When Chuck and Dina were not at school or work, they were in Ketona with family. The village of Ketona and Rushing Spring helped us raise our children. All children need a strong village because Jerri and I could not raise them without help. It is so important for parents to spend quality time with their children – it will make a difference.

Jerri and I always kept black history books available for Chuck and Dina to read. They both attended majority white high schools. I remember Dina being scolded in junior high school for speaking up about the history, she was being taught. In ninth grade, the white teacher told the class, there is no such thing as black people having Native American ancestry. Of course, Dina raised her hand and told us she said, "How are you going to say that, when I have Native American ancestry?" She went on to tell him our family history. The teacher became mad and Dina was required to write a report with proven facts — she did. Around the tenth or eleventh grade, she got mad again because it was Black History month and no Black History was being taught. She asked her teacher, "Why aren't you teaching us black history? You did not teach it before or after black history month." Again, another teacher got mad at Dina.

IF IT IS GOD'S WILL, I pray Jerri and I still have many, many years left to live. However, when I am long gone, I want my kids to still remember, you had better not ever be mediocre and you are required to be obedient. You will never settle for second best. We planted seeds in you both to excel.

I pray my grandchildren, Ashleigh and Jayla will not forget about family. I want my grandchildren to remember a family must always love each other. It does not matter where you live or who you will become, you will need family. When they visit Birmingham, I expect them to visit Rushing Spring.

I want Seth to always remember his great grandfather, Charles Sr. held a very special place in his heart for him. Sometimes, Daddy would get quiet and all of a sudden say, "I wonder what my Seth is doing." I wish Seth had more time with his Granddaddy. Daddy even spoke to me on how he regretted Seth lived so far away. It really hurt him that Seth would not get to really enjoy him like the other grandchildren.

To Ivan, I want you to be a man and not a wimp. Remember to slow down and listen. Lemuel, I want you to look up, quit looking back, be a man, and remember the grass is not always greener on the other side. Ezra, God has blessed your mind; therefore, let your mind be your guide and always shoot for the very best. The three of you must remember you will need your family and one day you will realize why God sent you into our lives.

To Jewaun, A.J. and Lamar, I truly love you. Tom, Bro, Tommy, and I need your help. The time is drawing near for you to help take care of the family's land. Even if a storm comes, you should go quickly to check on the land and help take care of things. If the church has an annual clean-up day, they need your help. It is time to continue the Avery legacy by being known as peaceful, strong Christian men, who make a positive difference within your community. Your future generations must remember you by your good work for the Lord. It is in your blood to become powerful leaders. Even if you decide to go to another church, you should give time and resources to Rushing Spring.

To all grandchildren raised by Eula and Charles Sr., I thank you that you are all living the way they wanted you to live. Nikia now has the youngest son. Nikia, remember the teachings of Ketona by providing instruction and discipline to your son, you must start early, if you do not,

Grandmommy will visit you in your dreams.

To my sister, Dot, you have always been a second mother to us and we do what you say we should do. I have always been closest to Doris Jean and I look forward to my daily morning calls. I am proud of my youngest sister, Carolyn for her academic and professional accomplishments. So to my sisters, I love you!

To my brother, Tom, yes, you are older, but I always felt that I am your protector. Since childhood, I always try to make sure you keep your cool because you are so quiet. I am protective of you because I never want anyone to upset you.

To my cousin, Victor, you already know God has your back. As you said, "You are mandated by God." It is no doubt you were born and chosen to preach and teach God's Word. You have always taken this position seriously. Never rush when making decisions and never be afraid to make your decision. Remember to always mean what you say and I know you have made Uncle Rec proud. Also, it is okay to use the word, "No" when dealing with members.

I want my church family to remember I truly love everyone. I try to know everyone and help everyone in need. The position of a Deacon is a very serious position and I try my best to uphold the teachings of God. My church family brings joy to my heart and I want to be remembered as being a mighty servant of God. Church, remember to always take care of our Pastor. He is growing and will need our prayers.

Chapter 12

What Time is it?

MY GRANDDADDY, CHARLES D. AVERY, SR., became ill in April 2013 and was hospitalized due to sharp stomach pains and then his lungs became irritated from years of suffering from asbestos. When he first went into the hospital, I knew immediately, he would soon die. I drove from Atlanta to visit him. Once I entered his hospital room, I walked to his bed and said, "I am here." He responded by saying, "Hey baby, what time is it?" I kissed his forehead and told him the time. For some reason, Granddaddy *always* wanted to know the current time. All of us would say, "Why does Granddaddy keep asking us what time is it?"

Even though, he repeatedly asked about the time, I was thankful he had enough strength to smile and speak with us. You could tell he was in pain, but he never really complained. All of my family was there at the hospital and no one did much talking, we just wanted to ensure he was okay. Church members and former neighbors from Ketona were in and out of his hospital room. I can see him now in the hospital bed wearing a hospital gown. I spent a few hours and told him that I was headed back to Atlanta. Prior to leaving for Atlanta, the doctors spoke about possible surgery and my father did not want Granddaddy to have surgery.

I left Birmingham thinking Granddaddy was not having surgery. Once I arrived to Anniston, my brother, Chuck called and said, "Go back to the hospital, Granddaddy is worse and will have surgery tonight." I got off on the next exit to head back to Birmingham. While driving, all I could think of was, "Granddaddy is ninety-five years old; how is he going to endure surgery?"

When I arrived to the hospital, my family, along with Deacon Roberson, was sitting in the hospital's waiting room and my cousin, Valerie informed me where Granddaddy was located, in order that I could see him before surgery. I kissed him and he said, "Baby, Granddaddy will be fine." I held back tears and kissed him again and again on his forehead. I stood there by myself until the hospital staff rolled him onto the elevator. Once the elevator doors closed, my tears started rolling. After I was able to stop crying, I went back into the waiting area with my family and together we prayed. After praying, we did not talk much, but of course, our cell phones were ringing non-stop.

Once the surgery was over, the surgeon came to speak with us. I recall him saying, "That man's insides look better than a young person." Family members responded by informing the doctor, "Granddaddy has never believed in smoking and drinking alcohol." The doctor shook his head and said, "I can tell." Granddaddy was sent to recovery and eventually, we were able to see him. We were thankful that he responded to us when we went to his bedside.

Granddaddy ended up, spending a few days in the hospital and went to the nearest rehabilitation center for therapy. While at rehab, he did more sleeping than therapy. He had no energy, but never complained. I recall telling my family, "You know Granddaddy loves to sleep so we should not be surprised."

After leaving the rehabilitation center, the decision was made that he and Aunt Bessie would live with my parents. Prior to him getting ill, Granddaddy stated where he would live, if he got sick. He even made legal arrangements for Aunt Bessie, just in case, my parents needed it and told us to keep quiet about it. The legal document gave permission to my parents to keep Aunt Bessie in his home with the appropriate medical staff even after his death. I always admired that gesture because he remained true to the promise, he made to Grandmommy and that was he would make sure Aunt Bessie would always have a place to say.

SINCE GRANDDADDY AND AUNT BESSIE were moving in with my parents, Chuck and I came home to help get the house ready. That was a job, but we did it. My brother broke down beds and moved furniture to get the house ready for them. Since Aunt Bessie was also ninety-five years old, we could not let her remain in Ketona by herself so she had to move in too with my parents.

When Granddaddy moved in, everyone's attention focused on him, even Aunt Bessie focused on Granddaddy. All of my life, Granddaddy experienced fainting spells and they continued. No one could ever figure out the cause of his fainting spells. We were so use to him fainting, but now since he was ill, it was a different feeling.

While at home in the hospital bed, he would faint and that was the worse feeling on Earth. All you could do was holler or hold your head down because deep down inside we all knew death was imminent. It got to the point where Daddy would just close the door and perform his magic on Granddaddy to bring him back conscious. One Sunday, Granddaddy fainted and once he regained consciousness, he started talking to my father. He said, "Baby Boy, I was gone that time." My father said, "I know Daddy, but you will see your ninety-sixth birthday." Granddaddy responded by saying, "You may have to carry me into my birthday" and Daddy replied, "I will." Anyone, who knows me, will tell you, I went into the other room and cried all over again.

It got to the point I was driving from Atlanta to Birmingham sometimes two or three times each week. Granddaddy spent most of his time sleeping and we played tons of gospel music. During the early morning hours after 3:00 am, Granddaddy always wanted to talk, probably because he slept all day like a baby. Since Granddaddy had my old bedroom, I slept on the sofa now when visiting.

On Monday, June 17, 2013, after 3:00am, I was awakened by the sounds of laughter and talking coming from Granddaddy's bedroom. Daddy was also smiling and talking, but Daddy's eyes guided me to Granddaddy's catheter. I could tell his kidneys were possibly beginning to shut down and I do not know why, but I said to myself, "Death is on the way." Daddy irrigated the catheter and I was trying to remain calm in front of Granddaddy even though he could not see us, he could feel when we were upset. Whenever I thought Granddaddy was in any type of pain, I just could not handle it. I always said my father should have been a nurse because he loves taking care of people and can remain calm while enduring stressful situations.

Although all this was going on, Granddaddy talked non-stop. While talking, he asked several times, "What time is it?" He said it so much that night, it got to the point, I turned to Daddy and whispered, "Why is Granddaddy asking the same question?" Despite how many times, he asked about the time, Daddy and I still responded by telling him the current time. Granddaddy always made me wait until 5:00 am to leave Birmingham driving back to Atlanta. On this particular morning, I wanted to leave at 4:00am, but once again, he made me wait until 5:00am. Our conversation that morning was different because he wanted to talk to the two of us about the future. His voice was not strong, but he meant business.

Granddaddy spoke about his expectations with our work in the church and he even spoke about Victor becoming the future Pastor of Rushing Spring. He gave Daddy specific instructions about the church and he was very firm with his tone of voice. I listened and then he went on to talk directly to me. He said, "All of you will not agree all the time, but you better eventually get over it. I mean it and stick together." I listened to his words and said, "Yes, Granddaddy." He even said, "Remember our project, you gotta get Ketona and Rushing Spring together to enjoy our memories. God will lead you and they will come. Do not forget anything I taught you and you must go to those places I spoke about – it is important. When you get back to Georgia, call us." I kissed his forehead and informed my Dad I would return Friday, June 21st.

GRANDDADDY'S BIRTHDAY was June 20th and my Aunts traveled from Michigan to celebrate with him. Our family friend, Wesley Bryant from Graysville, AL drove to our home with a birthday cake for Granddaddy. I called Granddaddy to say, "Happy Birthday." I reminded him that I was coming home the following day. My family spoke to me and told Granddaddy was enjoying, ice cream and tons of phone calls from all of his grandchildren, nieces, nephews, and anyone that knew him. He was happy and was even singing. His voice was not strong, but he gave it his all in his own way. He was so happy his youngest granddaughter, Nikia, who also traveled to Birmingham from Michigan was there in Birmingham. After his birthday, he continued to slowly decline and still asked, "What time is it?" Everyone still whispered, "Why is he asking about the TIME?"

When my aunts were not at our home with Granddaddy, they were in Ketona at Granddaddy's home to rest. We all knew he would never return to his home in Ketona and anyone, who knows my Aunt Doris Jean will tell you that when she travels to Alabama, she loves cleaning up and throwing out things. Granddaddy's home was not in bad shape, but it was now extra clean.

It is ironic how things happened before Granddaddy got ill, he told Daddy and I, the things we needed to get out of his home, such as old papers, pictures, and other family memorabilia. He wanted me to get his trunk out of the house along with a plastic bag that had papers in it. I had the trunk at my home, but when he was hospitalized I reminded Daddy to get the plastic bag with old papers and I told him exactly where it was located in Granddaddy's closet. I knew I had to get it before it was thrown away. Once Daddy found it on June 22nd, he called to let me know, "I found that bag." I then told Daddy to place the plastic bag inside my home in Birmingham.

Nikia and I went to Granddaddy's home, the afternoon of June 22nd and nothing felt the same. The inside of the house did not look the same and the outside of the house freaked us out. When we drove to the back of the home, the backyard was filled with black crows. We both felt that this was not a good sign and death was on the way. We did not cry, but we thought it was weird because we had never seen that many black crows in the backyard. After leaving Ketona, we went back to my parents' home to be with Granddaddy.

My Granddaddy always had a special place in his heart for our Mississippi family. We informed our Mississippi family of Granddaddy's downturn and our cousin, Jimmy hit the road coming to Birmingham for Granddaddy's birthday weekend.

I told Granddaddy that Jimmy was coming to visit for his birthday. Granddaddy was so happy and kept asking for Jimmy all day until he arrived. While lying in bed, he said, "Baby, call Jimmy and ask where he is and tell him to hurry up." I was obedient and got Jimmy on the phone. Jimmy said, "Tell Uncle Charles I am in Tuscaloosa, I am almost there."

The only visitor we had at the house when Jimmy arrived was my cousin, Donzetta. I heard Jimmy's truck outside and said, "Granddaddy, Jimmy is here!" Jimmy got out of the truck, greeted all of us and then went into Granddaddy's bedroom. Granddaddy and Jimmy greeted one another, held hands and my Granddaddy soon swiftly transitioned to heaven.

The hospice nurse had just gotten there and I think she and Daddy thought Granddaddy may be experiencing another fainting spell. When I saw them working on him, I yelled, "Granddaddy!" Daddy yelled and said, "Leave the room!" They continued to work with him, but on June 22, 2013, 8:10 p.m., Charles David Avery, Sr. was pronounced dead. Yes, I cried, but I remembered learning the hearing is the last thing to go when you die. I rushed to my Granddaddy and whispered the scripture from 2 Samuel 5: 10 that reads, "And David went on and grew great, and the Lord God of hosts was with him." After repeating this scripture, I kissed his forehead repeatedly and said, "Thank you, thank you, thank you for everything and I will keep my promise."

My Aunts and Uncle arrived back to my parents' home. They walked inside the home in silence. As a family, we had a prayer in Granddaddy's bedroom before the funeral home undertakers took his body. I think Jimmy was in shock because my Granddaddy waited on him to arrive before leaving this Earth. Granddaddy always had a special place in his heart from Jimmy's grandparents, Uncle Tommy and Aunt Sally, who once lived in Rushing Spring.

When the undertakers arrived to pick up Granddaddy, I did not want to see him placed in a body bag. My parents' home is small so Tommy and Daddy moved furniture in the den, in order for them to bring Granddaddy's body from his bedroom to the front door. When I saw the two men with the gurney, I went into my parents' room and shut the door. Mom followed behind me and quietly said, "Dina." I said, "Mom let me know when they are gone. I cannot handle seeing him like that."

AUNT DOT'S BIRTHDAY was the following day, but it was not much of a birthday celebration for her. All of us sat around in the living room, looking at each other and reminiscing about Ketona, Rushing Spring and our grandparents. I started to feel better once Chuck and Michelle arrived to Birmingham from Georgia. Eventually, Daddy and his siblings went into Granddaddy's bedroom to discuss funeral arrangements. Granddaddy funeral was held June 29, 2013, at Rushing Spring Baptist Church.

All of Granddaddy's children, grandchildren and great-grandchildren went to view his body on Friday morning. My father had not shown any emotion at home, but when he saw him in the casket, he walked over to the casket, touched him and greeted him by saying, "Hey Buddy." After that, he could not stop crying and Aunt Dot consoled him. After Daddy cried, it was a domino effect, the funeral home was filled with sobbing and many of us turned to Jayla because she was having a hard time.

The morning of the funeral, the family gathered at Granddaddy's home. As I walked onto the porch, I heard someone say, "The funeral home is almost to the church with Daddy." It hit me that Granddaddy had never been in church without family and I left to get to the church to meet his body. When the hearse pulled up, I stood at the door as they brought in his remains.

I remember Mrs. Byrd and an usher, Jeanette being there inside of the church. As they opened the casket, I was fine and Mrs. Byrd and I went to the casket. From there, a few relatives met at the old church to ring the church bell. The church bell is important to my family because we grew up hearing stories of how Granddaddy and his brothers were in charge of ringing the church bell before church service on Sunday mornings when they were kids. Standing near the bell along with me was Darryl, Seth, Jewaun, Jonathan and Jonathan's kids. It may have been a few others present, but I cannot remember. We each took a turn ringing the bell for Granddaddy, his parents, and siblings. Granddaddy's death marked an end to his generation, so ringing the church bell had many warm sentiments.

Tons of people gathered at the church and it was good seeing everyone. It was a beautiful homegoing celebration and we did not have all that screaming and hollering because although my Grandmommy is deceased, she would not stand for that. I could hear quiet sobbing from Granddaddy's sons and great-granddaughters. Granddaddy was dressed in a black suit, white shirt, and gold tie. For some odd reason, before his death, Granddaddy requested for his hands to be crisscrossed across his stomach at the time of his death and he died in this position. His hands were placed inside white gloves.

Granddaddy's sons wore black suits, white shirts, and a gold tie. His daughters, daughters-in-law, and granddaughters wore white dresses. We sat in the center aisle near the front of the church and our cousin, Donnie joined us on the front row. Donnie was our cousin, but Granddaddy loved him like a son. Donnie was very instrumental in ensuring Granddaddy was safe in his home when we were not in Ketona. Aunt Carolyn referred to Donnie as Granddaddy, "watchman" and we will never forget the love he still has for Granddaddy.

The repass after the homegoing celebration was held in Fultondale due to the large crowd and at that time our fellowship hall at the church was not complete. After the repass, we as a family went back to Granddaddy's home in Ketona. Before my Aunts left for Michigan, Aunt Dot announced that our grandmother wanted Valerie, Darryl, Greg, Tommy, Chuck, Nikia, and I to have the items in her China cabinet. All of a sudden, it hit me while sitting at the dining table that this was our last time as a family at our family home in Ketona and like I have said before, I cried again like a baby and my Aunt Mary tried to console me, but it did not help.

I had to stop and think if I feel this sad, just imagine how his children feel. Then, I had to thank God that we had him for so long. Daddy said it best, "I had my Daddy for over sixty years and that to me is a blessing." Yes, it is a blessing! I am now forty-two years old and I am just blessed for those God has sent my way. Everything I have ever endured, I am thankful because it made me who I am today. Granddaddy's death taught me that life still goes on, the clock does not stop ticking and we are only here for a season. I have learned that I must keep going because each day I am learning more about my purpose in life. Just like my forefathers, it is important for me to never let the legacy of Ketona, Rushing Spring and my family's legacy die and it will not.

Chapter 13

———

Bibb County

"Dina, you may need to go to Bibb County to do your research. I have given you the names of the slave masters, who owned the family. I have no idea, what you will run into, once you get there. God will lead you on what to do when you get to Bibb County."

– Charles D. Avery, Sr.

ALL OF THE DEATHS AND STORIES, I witnessed led me to the most profound moment of my life. While Granddaddy was alive, he told me, "Figure out how to get to the white Avery's then find out where our folks are buried. I bet you the whites will lead you to more information on us." Granddaddy told me the cities in Bibb County to visit and this really helped me to narrow down my search.

On August 4, 2014, I met face to face with the descendants of my ancestors' slave masters. The reason slave masters is plural is because in each slave masters' Last Will and Testament, you can read how they passed my family down to others within the same family. My family was considered their property.

June 23, 2014, I mailed via postal mail, a total of 83 letters that included my telephone number to churches and families located in Bibb County, AL. My letter was read at several churches and this letter led me to the descendants of the Avery slave masters.

My letter read as follows:

June 23, 2014

Greetings,

Dr. Dina Avery and Charles Avery, Jr. are currently researching African American family history. We are currently in need of speaking with anyone related to or has any knowledge of the Avery slave descendants of Bibb County. Even if you have artifacts and pictures related to the Avery slaves, we would love to speak with you.

If you have any valuable information, please call Dr. Dina Avery (205-xxx-xxxx). We truly thank you for assisting us with this project and many blessings to you all.

Thank you,
Dr. Dina Avery

Please note that for the sake of the slave masters' descendants' privacy, their names and restaurant location have been changed in this chapter, but I will give you all details on what occurred during my visit to Bibb County, AL. I received a phone call from a descendant of our slave masters. A neighbor of the white Avery's heard my letter read in their church and notified the Avery family. I received a phone call while driving in my car on my lunchbreak. The male voice on the other end of the phone said,

"This is Hector Avery and my neighbor told me you are researching your family history." I replied, "Yes sir." I proceeded to give him a brief synopsis of my book project. After doing so, Mr. Hector said, "Let's meet during the week because I will not be available on the weekend." I was shocked, but I remained calm. I said, "When do you want to meet?" The date was set for me to drive from Atlanta, GA to Bibb County on August 4, 2014.

When I got off the telephone, I called Daddy and said, "You will not believe, who I just spoke to." Daddy said, "Who?" My response, "We are headed to the Avery slave plantation to meet the descendants!" After telling Daddy, my conversation, he did not know what to say. Daddy said, "How did you find those folks?" I told him, "With the help of the church!"

I drove to Birmingham on August 3, 2014, and went to my parents' home. Together, Daddy and I reviewed notes from conversations with Granddaddy. Mom kept saying, "Y'all better be careful and do not stay too long."

On the morning of August 4, 2014, we started our journey to Bibb County, AL. We both were excited and I was a bit nervous because I did not know what to expect. I had tons of questions to ask and had all of my typed notes that dealt with my family history. Also, my father was helping me think. While riding, Daddy said, "Who will believe we are going to the master's plantation!"

Once we reached Tuscaloosa, AL, I knew we were almost there and a sense of urgency came over me. I wanted Daddy to put his foot on that gas pedal and drive faster. I did not drive because I was too busy reading my notes. In my mind, I was saying, "Daddy, just hurry up and get me there."

Before we arrived in Bibb County, we stopped at a gas station to call Mom and let her know we were almost there. Mom told us "Be careful and do not eat anything because you do not know these people." A short time after this conversation, Daddy and I arrived at the All of Us Restaurant. As we parked the car, I could not help, but giggle because the day was finally here.

Before I opened the car door, I looked around and saw two gentlemen getting out of a truck. Daddy looked at the two men and said, "That must be them." We then proceeded to get out of the car, to greet them. My father greeted them first and said, "Hi there, I am Charles Avery." I walked up behind Daddy and said, "And I am Dina Avery." Before I could thank them for meeting with us, the younger gentleman, Henry was standing in front of me and joyfully said, "Hello Cousins!" I quickly glanced at Daddy and smirked. The two men hugged me and it felt like I was walking in a cloud of fog to the restaurant and I deeply felt that everything was going to be okay. I sent Mom a text to let her know we were okay.

Together, we walked down the sidewalk into the All of Us Restaurant. Once we walked inside, everyone knew Hector Avery and Henry Avery. The petite, friendly waitress with southern charm greeted us and we sat at the table near the buffet table. I know this seems odd, but after our initial greeting, there was a sweet spirit surrounding us. These two men really were eager to help me with my project.

After being seated, I told Hector and Henry details surrounding Granddaddy. I explained how Granddaddy was our family's patriarch and he cherished our family history. Hector and Henry listened without interrupting and I explained how Granddaddy gave me orders to write a book related to our family history. Daddy pulled out his cell phone to show our family pictures. They took the time to look at each picture.

I had no idea, the two gentlemen brought a special family treasure for me. Henry pulled out a yellow folder with papers related to my ancestors. Henry handed the papers to me to read. Dad instantly saw the names, Sevie and Lide. In earlier chapters, Granddaddy told us about these two ladies. Lydia "Lide" Avery was my great-great-great-great grandmother and Sylvia "Sevie" was her daughter. I was later shown a document that coincided with what Granddaddy told me about the family's migration from North Carolina to Chesterfield County, South Carolina and then to Bibb County. I was sitting in total amazement at the papers in front of me.

After reading the papers, Henry explained how Hector's sister-in-law, Jean, who is now deceased gathered all the family's documents and information. She made copies for everyone and placed the copies into folders. Henry was very proud to have his yellow folder of family history.

After our initial discussion, the four of us proceeded to the buffet table to get our meat, three vegetables, and corn bread. When we returned to the table, we had more small talk to learn about each other. The older, Hector Avery wanted to know about my career. Hector turned to my father and said, "She is smart." Once we completed our meal, I thought we would say goodbye and go our separate ways, but Hector said, "I live on the Avery land, I want you to come by the house." I said, "Okay, thank you."

When we returned to our car, I called Mom and said, "We had lunch and headed to the plantation!" Mom said, "Oh Lord, don't y'all go, you do not know them." Daddy got the phone and said, "Jerri, we are fine and will call you back." Mom said, "Wait, did y'all really eat down there?" Daddy and I both said, "Yes!" I must say that the food was very delicious and reminded me of my family's cooking.

As we left the restaurant to drive to Hector's home, Daddy kept saying, "Wait until I tell Bro what we have witnessed today. Dina, I think these are good people!" Once we drove onto Hector's land, my mind did go back and try to imagine my family working the land as slaves. I refused to cry; I just took deep breaths and was ready to continue our discussions.

When I got out of the car, I took time to once more to look around at the land and houses. All of Hector's family still lives near him. He told me that at one time, the Avery's owned over 300 acres. During his childhood, Hector remembers white and black sharecroppers living on the land. In addition to the main house for his family, they had an additional ten houses for sharecroppers. According to Hector, everyone treated each other as family and they shared meals together at each other's homes. Hector said, "During the 1930s, it was not uncommon for us to go to our black neighbors' homes to eat and play because we were family."

Hector led us into the home he now lives in located on the Avery land. The house is immaculate and I promise you I did not see one drop of dust. The home feels like a cozy, happy home. It is not too big, but it is home. The four of us walked into the kitchen and sat at his wooden table. Before we started more discussions on family history, we bowed our heads to pray. Daddy prayed and I still could not believe I was sitting inside Hector's kitchen.

Henry proceeded to go to his house next door to make copies of the documents inside his yellow folder. While Henry was gone, Hector took me downstairs and around his home to look at family photos. Hector loves his family. Soon, Henry returned and greeted me again as Cousin Dina. Once Henry returned, Hector's daughters came home on their lunch break to meet me. Their names are Virginia and Mary.

Virginia and Mary came thru the door and first hugged their father and then greeted Daddy and me with smiles, open arms, and hugs. They were excited about my project and Virginia mentioned to me, "I told the ladies at work, I had to meet you." Virginia and Mary did not stay long, but they did not leave without taking photos with us and gave us more hugs. I could see in Hector's eyes, his daughters mean the world to him. Virginia and Mary adore their father just like I do my own father and grandfather.

The conversations continued around documents in the yellow, pocket folder. I am thankful Henry's Aunt Jean took the time to gather the documents. Two hours passed and we were still talking non-stop. I mentioned to Hector that Granddaddy informed me that train tracks are not far from him. He pointed to an area and told me train tracks used to be near his home but have since been removed.

Hector, also told me how the Avery's always loved horses. I responded by saying, "Granddaddy told me stories passed to him about the horses down here and how his grandfather trained horses. His grandfather loved riding horses." Hector said, "The family once had tons of horses and was always well-off financially." Hector honestly does not, in any way have hate in his heart despite differences we may possibly have. One thing, we have in common is genuine love, respect and admiration for each other that still exists today.

Once we finished talking at the kitchen table, Hector said, "Let's go for a ride." The four of us got into one car and drove around the Avery land. No one bothers the family because they really live in a world of their own – it is pure serenity. My promise to them is the way they live will stay like that and my family will not be coming down there to disturb them. My family often asks, "When are you taking me down there to visit?" My response is simple, "You can learn about them from this book and do not bother them. They do not want to be your tour guides." Once we returned to Hector's home, a man was walking up to the home asking to fish, and Hector's response was "not today." Daddy proceeded, saying, "Sir, I promise you and you have my word, I will not allow my folks to bother you because some of us know how to act and some do not." We all laughed and soon ended our visit.

Prior to getting into my car, I went to Mr. Hector and said, "You remind me a lot about Granddaddy because you keep your family together and you give tons of love." Hector gave me a hug like only a grandfather could give and I was not ready to leave, but it was time.

Hector and Henry are men that still love to hang on to their family ancestry, just like us. They talk about their ancestors, just like we do. They take care of their inherited family land and make sure their immediate family is taken care of, just like us. They have a sense of character and respect for humanity, just like grandparents taught all of us. Finally, they have love for God and love their Baptist church, just like us.

Since that visit in 2014, I spoke to Henry a few times over the telephone, whenever family history questions arise. Daddy also has spoken with Henry. Once I started writing the book, I contacted Henry and

Virginia to set a date for my return because I wanted the family to hear the unedited version of my chapter dedicated to them.

WE MET AGAIN on June 23, 2018 at the All of Us restaurant in Bibb County. Once Daddy and I arrived, we walked inside the restaurant and saw the Avery's sitting at a table behind the buffet table. On this visit, we met with Hector, Henry, Virginia, and Mary. I immediately noticed that Mary dyed her hair and said, "Something is different about your hair and I like it." Everyone still appeared to be happy and Cousin Hector opened his arms once again to hug me. He said, "I am glad you are here and it is so good to see you." We all chatted and talked about Daddy's bad knees. Daddy spoke about walking on the track each morning and Hector responded, "Cousin Charles, I think you had better take it easy." We all just laughed because Cousin Hector made a true statement.

Did you notice that the word, cousin was used? We do not know if we are blood-related to this set of Avery's, but there are other white Avery's, my blood has matched with. At this point, I am not even going to take the time to find out because it does not matter to us.

Now do I approve of their grandfather and their ancestors, owning my family all those years? My answer is a strong NO, but am I going to go around hating and belittling Hector just because his blood is connected to our slave owners. My response again is a strong NO. The only person I will never be around is one that has a heart filled with hate and rage.

While at the restaurant, I sat next to Henry while Virginia and Mary were in front of me. Daddy sat on the opposite side of me and Hector sat in front of Daddy. We had a deep discussion about our prayer life. Henry mentioned how he along with Virginia and Mary arise early each morning to pray before starting their day. Virginia mentioned, "Dina, you must wake up praying and put the whole armor of God on each day. When we are on the phone we have Bible Study and pray together." I have always had a strong prayer life, but when Mitzi mentioned putting on the whole armor of God, it stuck with me.

After we completed our meal, we went back to Hector's home to sit and talk. Everyone followed Hector into his home and this time we sat in the living room. Again, this house is spotless! You will not find a speck of dust in this house. During this visit, we spoke about the news and Hector wanted to catch up with what I had been doing. I updated him about my professional and church activities. Virginia and I spoke about recent travel and how it is important, just to enjoy life. I said, "Virginia, you must go to New York with me and have a good time." We still have not made this trip, but we will one day.

Once our visit ended, we did like our previous visit; we hugged and said our goodbyes. While on the road back home, I received a text message from Virginia. She sent her contact info and wrote how we need to keep in touch. Since that time, Virginia is my go-to prayer partner. Virginia genuinely loves me and I love her. I love it when she sends Bible study lessons and kind words. From time to time, I will send a book update and updates on additional white Avery's I have spoken with. While on this journey, I have spoken with other white Avery's from various States. I love learning from others and no one has been rude or cruel to me so far.

MY ANGEL ON THIS JOURNEY has been Dr. Baker, who is a well-known genealogist, who loves family history. Her family owned slaves and she is conducting research all the time. She has done a lot of research even on my ancestors. Her research is so detailed and organized. She can easily open up her documents and pull up her database.

Dr. Baker took time to show me the original documents and tax documents from the 1700s and 1800s. The tax papers were important to learning my history since slaves were considered property by this nation's government. Dr. Baker and I spent time just riding, locating the actual places where my ancestors possibly lived. Yes, we drove onto country roads with no trespassing signs. It is by the grace of God, no one harmed us on the back roads.

Dr. Baker and I plan more trips just to learn. We will expand our road trips to include more States that are linked to our family. One thing, Dr. Baker taught me was to listen to the voices of my ancestors. Whenever, we get a good clue, Dr. Baker will always smile and say, "The ancestors are speaking to us."

Although we have different skin tones, my family and inner circle are continuously expanding. It is sad that many in this country are divided because of our skin color. I am thankful that my village taught me to always be diverse. Everyone will never agree with everything we say or do, but we must be courteous, respectful and have a heart of love. To Hector, Henry, Virginia, Mary, Dr. Baker, and the rest of you that I have met, words will never express the gratitude I have for the love and kindness, you expressed to me while on this journey.

Chapter 14

Humbleness

I AM DR. DINA V. AVERY. I thank all of you, who took the time to read this book. Anyone that knows me will tell you that I work hard and I still have deep love for Ketona and Rushing Spring. To me, Ketona and Rushing Spring will always be one village. The majority of those, whom you have read about are now resting in their graves.

Our village shares so many fond memories because we lived as one family. I am forever thankful God led my parents to allow this village to help raise me. I still live a very simple life and remain humble because I have been taught the facts of life.

Humbleness is the key to success. My grandfather would always say, "You got to remain humble." Throughout my professional career, I have noticed that everyone cannot handle power and authority. I try to never get the "big head" because when you do, you will definitely fall. It is so important to treat people the way you want to be treated. I constantly pray for God to keep me humble.

Many reading this book, may say, "What is the purpose of this book?" The answer is simple, it is important for me to fulfill Granddaddy's dream of sharing our oral history and allowing the next generation to share in our precious memories.

To all of those, who have a dream that is burning within their soul, please follow your heart and fulfill your dream. Granddaddy deeply regretted not fulfilling his dream and now the book is published for you to read and he is no longer alive.

To all of the dreamers, please be careful, who you share your dreams with. Do not worry about anyone's opinion on what God has placed in your heart to do. Just do it!

In the course of writing this book, I had a close relative to speak, very firm with her words and say, "Only those close to you, will care to read this story. This is the problem with most authors." I listened to her critiques, but I am thankful she expressed what was really on her heart. Her conversation was centered on selling numbers. She ended by saying, "I hope the book is a blessing to *those*, who decide to read it."

I feel if this book sells a total of five copies, I will be overjoyed because I completed an overdue dream that became my goal to complete. It is not about fame, but all families and neighborhoods all over the globe should chronicle their history. I love hearing and learning from others.

Whenever my family and I get together now, all we do is talk about the great memories we shared in our village. We have so much fun talking about 729 Pine Hill Road and we spend hours just reflecting back as a family. It is so important for families to laugh together and keep building upon those memories.

My family no longer owns 729 Pine Hill Road, but God sent a very nice family to purchase the home. They still allow my family to visit because they understand how special the home is to us. I still have not gone inside the home since the new owners moved in, but they allowed Daddy to take pictures of the new remodeling that was recently completed.

Each week, I drive by 729 Pine Hill Road to attend church at Rushing Spring. Sometimes, when I drive by, I still glance at Granddaddy's window where he kept his curtain pulled back until it was time for him to go to sleep. Today, the curtain is always closed, but I know his spirit is still lingering within our village.

WHEN I NOW DRIVE ON LONG STREET, I truly miss the woman, who had one of the greatest impacts on my life. Her name was LeeAnna Crumpton Holder. Ms. LeeAnna ruled everyone in Ketona and she hardly ever left her yellow house. Ms. LeeAnna ruled us by yelling from her screened-in front porch and calling us on the telephone. She always called our home before and after the soap operas. Ms. LeeAnna would call and say, "Eula, did you see what happened on the *stories?*"

I recall when I was around eight or nine years old, having fun while riding my brand new bike given to me by Aunt Odell. I had no idea, Ms. LeeAnna was watching me from her front porch. When I went inside for the day, the phone started to ring. I heard Grandmommy pick the phone to say, "Hey LeeAnna." Soon Grandmommy handed the phone to me. Ms. LeeAnna spoke to me very firmly and said, "I saw you riding that bike all day and that means you have not studied. I know Jerri left you workbooks down there. Now, get to the kitchen table and do your work!" I listened and did exactly what she told me to do. Grandmommy smiled and said, "I guess LeeAnna got us told today, you had better do your work. I just wanted you to enjoy your new bike."

I only remember seeing Ms. LeeAnna leave her home two times. The first time was to attend the funeral of her husband, Joe Holder, who was the brother-in-law to my Aunt Lottie Mae. While Ms. LeeAnna was attending the funeral, Grandmommy and I sat at her house since no one would be home. Grandmommy said, "Dina, we gotta watch LeeAnna's house since no one will be there." I just looked at her and smiled because Ms. LeeAnna's house is directly across the street from the church where her husband's funeral was being held. No one would have been bold enough to bother Ms. LeeAnna's home.

The second time I saw Ms. LeeAnna leave home, I was eleven years old. Ms. LeeAnna was sitting at my grandparent's kitchen table to watch the house while all of us attended Grandmommy's funeral at Brownsville United Methodist Church. Ms. LeeAnna was sitting there stricken with grief from losing a close friend. I walked over o her and all she could do was squeeze my hand, look into my eyes and she had no words.

When Grandmommy died in 1989, Ms. LeeAnna still remained close to all of us. Chuck, Tommy, and I visited her every Sunday after dinner at Granddaddy's home. All of her children and really people in the neighborhood would be sitting in Ms. LeeAnna's bedroom after Sunday dinner. Everyone would be excited to get our spot on her bed. I always got to hold her granddaughter, Denita. All we did in Ms. LeeAnna's bedroom was to listen to her talk and laugh. Ms. LeeAnna had a way of smiling with those big cheeks and you could not help, but smile too.

During the week, I could sometimes catch Ms. LeeAnna by herself in her bedroom. When we had one-on-one talks, she often said, "You will do well in life and you had better not ever forget this place. Do you hear me?" I would always smile at her and say, "I promise you, I will never forget about this place." Looking back, it was like she was looking into my future. Ms. LeeAnna's sister, Doll also spoke words of wisdom to me.

Grandmommy and Ms. LeeAnna did not allow me to play with all of the kids in Ketona. They always protected me because I was always very timid with a tender heart. Yes, I still cry over anything. They were always quick to tell me, who I could and could not play with. My cousin, Brian Shelton was a playmate, who often visited so we could ride our bikes together on my grandparents' long driveway.

YOU READ MANY SPEAKING ABOUT GRANNY. I was a child when Granny died and people in the neighborhood cared for her during her last days on Earth. We made sure Granny was loved and felt comfortable. My job was to get on Granny's bed, wipe her forehead and say, "Granny, we love you so much." Granddaddy would be there too and together, we cleaned Granny's slop jar that was next to her bed because even in 1985, she did not have indoor plumbing.

I remember Grandmommy calling Cousin Mattie Pearl late at night saying, "Daddy is dropping me off at Granny's, I will see you there." I do not remember Granny's funeral, but I remember hearing Granddaddy say, "Dina, Granny died." I looked at Grandmommy and we all silently cried. Our Granny lived a long life. Even though she did not have biological children, she was midwife to the baby boomer generation of Ketona and our village of all ages cared for her up until her death.

WHEN I WAS NOT IN KETONA, I spent time in Rushing Spring with Auntie Senie. I would watch my aunt grab a broom to sweep from the top of the hill at Rushing Spring and down to the bottom of the hill. She had to be over eighty years old and she never wanted any help while sweeping.

When we were younger, after Sunday School, my cousins, Victor, DeWayne, Jewaun, and I would go to Auntie's house. On this particular Sunday, she had just baked a cake. The boys were in the dining room eating cake and I was in the adjacent living room. A mouse came out of nowhere; I screamed and jumped up on the chair. The boys grabbed their cake and did not stop eating while they stood on the chair.

On another Sunday after church, we beat Auntie home. She always left the door unlocked because our family was in and out of her house on Sundays since she lived by the church. DeWayne found a pistol and thought it was a toy gun. DeWayne, Victor, and I took turns firing the gun in the front yard. We had no idea the gun was the real! Auntie soon came home and we told her to fire the gun too. After she fired the gun, Auntie said, "Oh Lord, where did you find this? This gun is REAL!" Each one of us did not know what to say and we looked at DeWayne. Fortunately, we did not kill ourselves on that day.

AT RUSHING SPRING BAPTIST CHURCH, we still have good, old fashioned church. Our church is a Bible-based, teaching us and we care about each other. As a kid, I can remember it being funny and exciting when someone would catch the Holy Spirit and start shouting at church.

Now, I am the one getting the Holy Ghost and hollering "yeah, yeah, preach" when the Spirit is high. I still can recall being very young, maybe in pre-school and our fifth Pastor, preached a sermon on the prodigal son and he walked the aisle while preaching the Word.

Let me tell you, all I know is that on that Sunday, the church was going wild. When the preacher got to the part when the prodigal son returned home, people were on their feet almost leaping over the pews. Granddaddy was yelling in my ear, "Yeah, preach son, preach!" Even Daddy was waving his hands, yelling "Preach, come on, preach." Granddaddy whispered to me to "sit up and listen baby" and eventually he was on his feet praising God right along with everyone else. I had so many questions going through my mind like, what is happening here. I was in total amazement. As a family, we still speak about that sermon.

In our church, if Sister Wessie Howard, who was the Mother of the Church, got the Holy Ghost, the preacher had to be telling the truth sent by God Almighty. Sister Howard would sit on the second row to the right of the aisle with her great-grandson. Sister Howard did not get the Holy Ghost all the time, but when the Holy Ghost came, it took over her entire body. Sis. Howard would first grab her hands tight, then start clapping repeatedly real fast, and then she would verbally say, "Thank you Jesus, thank you Jesus, thank you Jesus." She never yelled, but it was real. As kids, we would watch Sister Howard because deep down inside, we knew she was having an out of the body experience and we all felt whatever she was feeling.

Sis. Howard was the sister to my grandfather's best friend, J.T. I can see the ushers in my mind now running down the aisle to take care of Sis.

Howard. Back then, the Ushers Ministry wore navy blue dresses, with a white lapel and two rows of white buttons. Their dresses came down to their knees and they wore thick, white stockings. It was their protocol to always take Sister Howard's eyeglasses off and use the fan with the funeral home advertisement to cool her down. Nowadays, they say "don't fan out the fire." I honestly do not think that Sister Howard even noticed them taking off her eyeglasses because she really had the Holy Ghost inside her body.

Back then, we also had the Nurses Guild and they wore all white with white nursing hats, white stockings, and those classic, white nursing shoes with a thick sole. Aunt Lois Avery and cousin, Vivian Booker were on the Nurses Guild and would be on standby with a small, brown bottle. The brown bottle was known as smelling sauce. They used it, if you passed out and yeah, the smelling sauce worked because once they put it to your nose, it made you jump up. I still do not know what was in that brown bottle.

I CAN STILL REMEMBER Granddaddy's dad, Rector Alexander Avery, who everyone called Papa or Papa Alec. A lot of my cousins called him Papa, but he was my Paw-Paw. On Sundays, we always parked near his home. Even in his nineties, Paw-Paw always kneeled at the altar to pray. Paw-Paw loved Rushing Spring. I do not remember Paw-Paw talking much, but I always would hold his hand when he walked up and down the hill at Rushing Spring.

I still remember the events leading up to Paw-Paw's death. Granddaddy would stay in Rushing Spring at night when Paw-Paw became ill. We visited more than usual and the house was filled with family. Paw-Paw was not saying much, just lying in bed.

While at my parents' home, the phone rang and someone on the other end told my father, Paw-Paw died. Daddy said to us, "Get your clothes on, Papa just died." Mama hollered, "Dina and Chuckie hurry up!" We dressed and went to Rushing Spring. I remember seeing people and cars everywhere. I remember getting out of my parents' car to find my Granddaddy. Granddaddy took me by the hand and led me to see my Paw-Paw. I did not cry and Granddaddy's said, "Touch my daddy, it is okay." I looked up at Granddaddy and I touched Paw-Paw's hand. Granddaddy then kneeled down and put his arm around me while we stared at Paw-Paw. Granddaddy said, "Dina, do not forget this moment and do not forget that man right there." My response at the age of four years old, "Granddaddy, I will never forget my Paw-Paw." Granddaddy picked me up and together we stared at the head of our family before leaving to go to the front porch. When the funeral home arrived to get his body, everyone went toward the front yard in silence and the men of the family went toward the hearse and spoke to the funeral home attendants. The funeral home attendants along with Paw-Paw's son carried his body and placed it inside the hearse.

SUNDAY WHEN I WAS A CHILD, were days to spend with God and family. Each Sunday, we had a full course meal and Aunt Bessie always provided sweet tea. My extended family really never had to visit from house to house because even today, we see each other at Wednesday Night Bible Study, Thursday night choir rehearsal, Sunday worship service, church meetings and other church events. We catch up with each other while sitting inside church. If we are not sitting close to each other, we will text one another and wave. We even text my cousin, Victor to say "hello" while he is sitting in the pulpit.

We now have a new church edifice at the bottom of the hill, but I still go back on top of the hill near our old church sometimes to pray and reflect back. I remember when it was announced that Victor would serve as our seventh Pastor, he too went back to the top of the hill, where it all started to pray, and give thanks. Recently, Verbin Jr. said, "I look out in our woods and think of our family that is gone all the time. I can see Mama Shelly fishing with us. God knows I am thankful. Those were the good old days."

Again, please take time to enjoy your elders, enjoy those you love and pull out your family photo albums. Start planning more Sunday dinners and just enjoy each other. I hope you remember to do that. Life should be about celebrating and making memories that will be cherished forever.

Each day, I am learning to slow down and enjoy the simple pleasures in life. When I walk outside, I sometimes will stop to take a deep breath and look around to enjoy the leaves blowing, the smell of green grass and the sound of birds chirping. As a kid in Ketona, Granddaddy would always get excited when a red cardinal or bluebird was in the backyard. I can hear him now, "Dina, come look at the birds. Hurry before they fly over the tracks." Now when I see these birds in the morning, I cannot help, but smile because I have eyes to see and so many blessings surround me.

Before I end, I must thank my forefathers for taking a chance on jumping the trains. If they did not have the courage to do so, I would not be sitting here writing this story. Just think, many relationships that still exist are all because of them.

Acknowledgements

I SINCERELY THANK GOD for providing Granddaddy the vision for this book project. This book is a precious gift that we can forever cherish. The memories of Ketona and Rushing Spring that we once knew, will now never die.

To Mom, Dad and Chuck, we are one heck of a team and I love you tremendously. Mom and Dad, thanks for allowing Ketona and Rushing Spring to take part in my upbringing. I am truly grateful and thankful. Dad, I know how protective you are of our original family records from the 1800s, thanks for letting me keep the records for a few days (smile).

A huge thank you to everyone, who assisted me with this book project. Thanks so much for providing your prayers, love, time, input and support. Words will never describe my gratitude for your kindness. To those closest to me, thanks for putting up with my busy schedule and long work hours. To my A-1, thanks for your patience, attentiveness, and love.

Note from the Author

———

THIS BOOK PROVIDES ORAL HISTORY passed down from our forefathers to my paternal grandfather, Charles D. Avery, Sr. My grandfather provided details based upon what he could remember from personal experiences, encounters and conversations. The past residents of Ketona and Rushing Spring also provided their recollections based upon personal experiences. Only those names provided to me by my grandfather were asked to participate in this book project.

I did review U.S. Census Bureau records and other ancestral records to gain insight on details related to genealogical details provided to me by my grandfather and others. Dr. Baker was helpful in reviewing with me tax records and other county records related to my ancestors. The Jefferson County Department of Health, Vital Records Department located in Birmingham, AL was a valuable resource in locating records related to my ancestors – thank you Janica Davis your patience and guidance.

ABOUT THE AUTHOR

DR. DINA V. AVERY was born in Birmingham, AL and spent most of her childhood in the Ketona and Rushing Spring communities. After receiving, her undergraduate degree from the University of Montevallo, she completed four additional graduate degrees. Dr. Avery is an experienced researcher, lecturer, and mentor. *Jumping the Train* is her first published book.

www.dinaavery.com

Instagram: @dr.dinaavery

Made in the USA
Columbia, SC
04 September 2019